Self-knowledge, as Dr Chesser explains,
is the key to the art of purposeful living.
You must know yourself before you can
understand other people. And since
human relationships underlie almost
all of our actions, self-awareness is as
vital to you as eating or sleeping. That
is the starting-point of this unique book
which covers every area of life, from
childhood to old age.

Also by
Dr Eustace Chesser

SEXUAL BEHAVIOUR
UNMARRIED LOVE
YOU MUST HAVE LOVE
KNOW YOURSELF
GROW UP AND LIVE
SEX AND THE MARRIED WOMAN

and published by Corgi Books

Eustace Chesser

Who Do You Think You Are?

CORGI BOOKS

TRANSWORLD PUBLISHERS LTD

A National General Company

WHO DO YOU THINK YOU ARE?

A CORGI BOOK 0 552 08805 6

Originally published in Great Britain by
W. H. Allen & Co. Ltd.

PRINTING HISTORY

W. H. Allen edition published 1970
Corgi edition published 1971

This book is set in Baskerville 11/12 pt.

Corgi Books are published by Transworld Publishers, Ltd.,
Cavendish House, 57–59 Uxbridge Road, Ealing,
London, W.5.

Made and Printed in Great Britain by
Richard Clay (The Chaucer Press), Ltd., Bungay, Suffolk.

CONTENTS

Know thyself: this is the great object.

LUCIUS SENECA
(Roman) 4 B.C.–A.D. 65

He who knows himself, knows others.

CALEB COLTON
(English) 1780–1832

*Perception of yourself. Is not that plain enough before your face?
Then what more is there that you need to know?*

DANDEMIS
(Indian) Third century B.C.

CHAPTER ONE

WHAT'S THIS ALL ABOUT?

By way of introduction, let me explain my purpose in writing this book. I believe I can best do so by sketching in broad outline the wider issues which we shall be discussing.

But before going further I must make it clear that I am *not* writing one of those treatises which guarantee to show how you can 'Have a body like mine', 'Get rich quick', 'Fool all the people all the time', 'Get the girl next door', etc. You know the sort of book I mean? Well, this is not going to be one of those. I think I should mention in passing that it isn't about sex, either. I have already written so many books on that subject that I feel you should be reassured—this is not yet another.

What kind of book *is* it, then? To answer as briefly as possible, I'd like to quote Henrik Ibsen. He wrote: *So to conduct one's life as to realise oneself—this seems to be the highest attainment possible to a human being. It is the task of one and all of us, and most of us bungle it.*

I think most of us are *still* bungling it. And I believe I know why and how, and that I can help a large number of people to get things straightened out.

You will have noticed that I am not writing in either a formal or clinical manner. This is deliberate, because I am not writing for psychologists, nor for literati, nor even for the critics. I am writing for *people*, ordinary people.

It is the ordinary person who, if he gives no thought or planning to his relationships with others, all too easily becomes confused by the stresses and complications of everyday life. It is this ordinary person—who might be you—who finds he is unable to do justice to himself and his relationships. At that point he may well find himself on the psychiatrist's couch.

I believe that through this book I can help you to lock a few stable doors before the horses bolt. Of course, what I wish to propound here is largely the result of many years' clinical experience as a consultant psychiatrist; but I am not writing *as a psychiatrist*, and I intend as far as is possible to avoid using psychiatric terms. *I am addressing the man in the street in the hope that what I say will help him to remain in the street, and not become the man in the psychiatrist's waiting-room.*

(I use the term 'man' in the generic sense; I am not, of course, addressing myself exclusively to the male sex. Practically everything I say applies equally to men and to women, but where I need to refer to one or other separately, I shall make it clear in the text.)

No more preamble. Let us move on and try to establish a pattern for discussion.

Health

Good physical health is essential to the living of a full life. It is just as important as mental health, and since it is—generally speaking—well within the powers of most of us to see that our bodies are properly cared for, we should perhaps make this our first objective.

I am not suggesting that we should become faddists or hypochondriacs. This would be a symptom of partial

2

failure in mental health, an imbalance in what should be the *overall* objective—physical *and* mental well-being. The old-fashioned 'hearty' doctrine of 'take care of the body and the mind will look after itself' is as fallacious as its converse would be. Physical and mental well-being are complementary to each other, and a breakdown in one must affect the other, even though we may not see the relationship between them.

Now this is not a medical textbook. There are plenty of those on the market, and the advice of a doctor is easily obtained. Even without such assistance any reasonably intelligent person knows perfectly well that if he smokes too much, drinks too heavily, doesn't get enough sleep or exercise or does not take reasonable precautions against the ills which threaten his bodily welfare, he will suffer in one way or another. So when I say we should make physical health the first objective, I am not asking you to do more than put a little common sense into practice.

The direct link between physical and mental health means that each affects the other, and both are part of a whole. For instance, it won't help you in your relations with other humans to be able to demonstrate bright eyes, an upright carriage and enormous reserves of stamina if, within a few minutes of speaking to a hitherto admiring audience, they either fall asleep or rush for the door.

If you're going to get any satisfaction out of life, people have got to like you.

They won't *all* like you, however good a job you make of it. (We will discuss this point in detail on p. 26.) But the people who might like you certainly won't if you don't allow yourself to like them, if you're so uninterested that you don't even make the effort. Nor will they like you if you're so wrapped up in yourself that

3

you don't have the time or ability to show as much interest in them as you'd like them to have in you. Human relationships are reciprocal and mutual. And most—if not all—human relationships can be studied.

A healthy mental approach to other people can be taught and acquired. It may in a minority of cases 'come naturally', burgeon without conscious effort along with a person's growth and development, but those in whom that natural gift is sown are both rare and fortunate; they certainly do not need the help of a book like this. But if you are one of the ninety-nine people out every hundred who *do* need help with their personal relationships, you can be taught the art and as you practise you will get true satisfaction from the efforts which you'll be making. Finally you will succeed, and will be putting the principles into practice as a matter of course, effortlessly, because they will have become part of the way you naturally behave.

When you are making the most of your relationships with others, you will have gone a long way towards making the most of yourself.

Horse-power

If you imagine you can do more than make the most of yourself, you might as well volunteer to become an astronaut. You're reaching for the moon already, so while you're at it why not become a professional?

Put it another way. When you're driving a $1\frac{1}{2}$-litre family saloon and you stop at traffic-lights beside a 3-litre GT job, if you have any sense at all you won't try to beat the big fellow across the intersection. If you do, as likely as not you'll start by blowing a gasket and finish up looking and feeling stupid.

It's just the same with people. We each have a certain

4

potential, calibre or capacity—call it what you will. We must know what that potential is—in other words, we must make a full and honest stock-taking of our personal assets and liabilities—before we can decide just where to set our targets.

Surely this makes sense. If you're a crack shot and equipped with a high-powered sporting rifle, you'll get little satisfaction from hitting a bottle at 25 yards. On the other hand, if you're a lousy shot and all you have to shoot with is an airgun with a wobbly front sight, you would be better advised to start by trying to hit a barn door at half that range.

The objective should be the maximum within your ability. Anyone can do what's easy for him, but, to derive real satisfaction, his achievement should demand total effort, full use of all resources and strengths. If you set your sights lower than you have power to reach, it is a waste of time and talents.

If you extend yourself to the limit, the limits will seem to expand, the boundaries will be edged back while your potential grows. If you stick to what comes easily, to what you've managed in the past instead of what you *could* do now, your boundaries won't expand; if anything they will shrink. If on the other hand you set the target clearly beyond your range, that is if you go for unattainable objectives, you'll miss every time —and what good will that do you? I'll tell you what *harm* it will do: it will frustrate you, disturb your mental health, and since mental and physical health are interdependent, it could very well, in the end, seriously handicap you. True, none of us is going to escape death—but we might as well try to die happy!

A man must have a sense of humour and a sense of direction, a determination to fulfil himself and achieve his goal. To live his life successfully and with satisfaction, he must be certain that the success he is aiming for is not just a remote possibility, but is a perfectly feasible probability. If he goes about it on the lines I have just sketched, this need be no pipe-dream, but a practical blueprint for the purposeful and positive direction of one's life. So—*to make the most of yourself—know yourself!*

People

No man lives entirely by himself: he lives in communication with others, and with the various parts of himself. His relationship with every person he meets, casually or otherwise, affects his own well-being and theirs. There can be few whose lives have not been affected, perhaps even dramatically changed, by a 'chance' encounter which at the time seemed totally unimportant. When we are aware of such an experience, how can we fail to understand that every single relationship with another human being is worth a full measure of respect and care?

Never was this more obvious than in the present age of swelling populations and increasing social and economic pressures—the highly organized and highly competitive society in which, whether we like it or not, our paths are set.

The only way to 'opt out' is by partial or total self-destruction. Since, fortunately, only a minority are likely to choose that alternative, it is not a subject I shall dwell on here.* I am addressing those who intend to stay in the swim—or, if you prefer it, in the rat race. But I believe it is more difficult—that it requires greater awareness, knowledge and technique—to

* A full study of the subject is contained in *Why Suicide?* by Eustac Chesser (Arrow paperback, 1968).

become and to remain a 'whole', contented and successful person, in this latter half of the twentieth century than ever it was before.

It seems strange that so little has been written in the form of *practical* guidance. One could fill whole libraries with books on philosophy and psychology published in the last decade or two, and of course there is much to learn from the vast majority of them. But they are nearly all written on general lines—they impart information, theory, knowledge. For this to be of practical use in our daily lives, we have not only to absorb the knowledge but (*a*) to find out how we can put it to work, and (*b*) to be capable of selling it to others. For some people this can be very difficult—particularly for those who lack insight, awareness of their own and other human beings' motivations. But just as we can be taught to drive a car without knowing exactly how its engine works, we can be taught how to conduct our relationships with other people without necessarily having to appreciate the conscious and unconscious motivations, the reasons why all of us act and react as we do.

Obviously it would be better if we *did* have such knowledge—there's no doubt that the best drivers do know what makes their cars function and respond to each touch of the controls. But lack of it need not restrict the vast majority of averagely intelligent people from adopting outlooks and attitudes—of 'going through the motions'—which will result in their living far more effectively and satisfactorily.

That is the aim with which I shall be concerning myself in this book.

There are, of course, a lot of what people call 'self-improvement' books about. Indeed, some of them have been 'about' for some years. But when one looks into their content one finds that 90 per cent of it is aimed at telling the reader how to make more money or build a bigger business. Well, I'm certainly not averse to *my* readers getting rich too, but I must make it clear that it is not my object in this book to concentrate on commercial or career angles, or anything else in that narrow sense. It's undeniable that by

Living more fully
Relating your personality purposefully to other people's
Fulfilling yourself in human terms

you will succeed to the same extent in each separate area of your life, including business. But this is incidental. What I'm concerned with here is the whole business of living. I'm addressing people who want to be people. Even—and here's an ambitious step forward—people who want to be *happy* people.

How to use this book

As you read you will probably think there is a great deal to try to take in at once. You may say, 'How on earth can I remember all these do's and don'ts?'

The simple answer is that in one reading you can't. When you're starting to learn anything, you *don't* take in everything at once. But as you have more lessons and more practice, each detail fades as a separate action and becomes part of the whole process.

Obviously this takes a little time. You won't absorb all the lessons of this book in one quick reading. So when you've come to the last page, don't throw it away. Keep it somewhere near you, spend a few minutes each evening re-reading it. Check what you've done each day against the principles we've enunciated. Ask yourself,

'Did I handle that situation as well as I might have done?' 'Could I have managed it more effectively?'

If you can't manage to do this every day, do it every *two* days—or once a week. *But keep at it*. Before long, you won't need to refer to the book any more. You will know and understand the principles so well that you'll be applying them naturally in your dealings with other people.

When you've reached that stage, you can afford to lend it to someone else. Until then—hang on to it, and use it!

CHAPTER TWO

YOU CAN ONLY PLAY THE HAND YOU'RE DEALT

The dealer flips the cards around the table, and the players pick up their hands. But the game doesn't start till each player has checked his cards, assessed their possibilities, and decided how he is going to play them.

Now in this analogy, the individual cards represent your strengths and weaknesses, abilities and limitations, and the complete hand represents your personality. Each of us is dealt a hand at birth. By adolescence and adulthood some of the cards have changed: we've discarded some, and replaced them with others. By the middle years of life, the set of cards will have changed again, for only such things as cabbages stand still, unaltered by experience, events and the influence of fellow beings.

So the hand you hold today is not completely identical with the one with which you started. It doesn't matter what stage you have reached in your growth, I am addressing you as you are now. Whether you've just scooped your cards off the table or whether you've changed or rearranged them, you can still check your cards, assess and reassess your hand, plan and replan how to make the best of what you've got.

Perhaps the analogy has gone far enough. But before I leave it, think of this: if a man gives that much consideration to the playing of a simple game, shouldn't he give as much or more forethought to each move in his game of life?

Self-analysis

A man lives from the time he is born until the day he dies, and in that space of time, he plays, as Shakespeare says, many parts. In each he has to relate his own personality to the personalities of other human beings. To do so purposefully and effectively he must first understand himself.

There are of course hundreds of different facets and ingredients to what we call 'personality'. In fact each of us is made up of many personalities, but I shall confine myself for present purposes to just two of them. The first is *maturity*; the second is introversion/extraversion.

How mature are you?

What does maturity mean? In a nutshell, I'd put it like this:

(a) The mature man is able to adapt himself to circumstances—when to do so is justified—and is able to refuse to do so when it is unjustified.

(b) He is able to face facts as they are and not as they exist in his imagination.

(c) He recognizes he must have some regard for others; he does not exist by himself.

(d) He is reasonable in his judgement of others and tolerant in his attitudes.

(e) He is able to think objectively, having rid his mind of preconceived ideas and blind prejudices.

(f) He should, as far as possible, be the master and not the victim of his irrational urges.

On the other hand:

(a) The immature man is irrational in his attitudes.

(b) He has an excessive fear of failure and finds it difficult to accept the challenge of life.

(c) He tends to approach adult situations in an infantile manner.

(d) He is, in the main, narcissistic and self-centred.

(e) He finds it difficult to give credit to others, but demands the limelight for himself.

(f) He finds it difficult to stand on his own two feet for he remains excessively dependent on others.

Now see if you can answer the following questions honestly. (If you answer them *dis*honestly you'll be fooling only yourself, and if you do that it's a waste of time reading this book.)

(1) Do you think childhood is the happiest time of life?

(2) Do you worry about getting older?

(3) Does the thought of making your Will upset you?

(4) Do you fuss about your health?

(5) Do little things 'throw' you?

(6) Do you make up flattering stories about yourself?

(7) Do you day-dream about winning the pools?

(8) If someone upsets you do you feel you must even the score?

(9) Do you remember old grievances?

(10) Do you attribute your failure to bad luck?

(11) Do you become depressed after a disappointment?

(12) Do you think you are better than others believe you to be?

(13) Are you afraid to express unpopular views?

(14) Does it upset you when you cannot get your own way?

(15) Are you interested only in yourself?
(16) Are you much influenced by advertisements?
(17) Do you enjoy hearing of other people's misfortunes?
(18) Do you indulge much in sexual fantasies?
(19) Do you believe that sex is the only thing that matters in life?
(20) Are you superstitious?

Score one point for each 'yes'. If to some questions your answer is 'sometimes' or 'only under certain circumstances' give yourself half a point.

A score of 20 would indicate extreme immaturity. A score of nought would suggest that you were either extraordinarily mature or (more likely) thoroughly dishonest. Answer the questions again—*truthfully*!

However, the point of issue is that of *excess*. Most people have thought at some time that it would be decidedly pleasant to have a big win on the pools, but this is not the same as wallowing in day-dreams of doing so. If you didn't think *you* might win, you wouldn't fill in your coupons. That is one thing, but if you allow the dream of winning to pervade your waking hours you are wasting your life in fantasy.

Similarly, I know that the man who tells me he has never indulged in sexual fantasy is not speaking the truth, but it is equally true that the adult personality does not dream constantly of sex, nor does he continuously stimulate himself with pornography.

How should I describe a person whom we should regard as mature?

(1) He faces facts.
(2) He does not ignore reality, either in his life surroundings or in his own limitations.
(3) He knows there is such a thing as luck, but that it is up to him whether he succeeds or fails.

(4) Within the limits of his capabilities, he is self-reliant.

(5) His is a balanced personality, so that he can take the unexpected—good or bad—in his stride.

(6) He seeks no escape into an irretrievable past nor into an imaginary future.

(7) He knows that he is living in a changing world, that he must keep up with it and not expect it to change for him.

(8) He shows interest in what goes on around him, and concern for other people.

(9) He hasn't time to be bored.

(10) His experience has given him principles which he follows, but he remains flexible enough to adapt to circumstances.

If you've been honest with yourself, you know how well (or how badly) you measure up to those standards of maturity. Perhaps your conclusions suggest there is room for improvement?

If you can't answer 'yes' to that question, you needn't read further. If you believe you have nothing to learn, nothing I can say will make any difference. But if you are honest you will admit the points of weakness in yourself, and it is only when you admit these to yourself that you *can* do something about it.

The very fact of recognizing these points is an advance in self-awareness, and that in itself is the first step towards self-improvement.

Now we come to the second important aspect of personality.

Introvert or extravert?

The introvert looks inward at himself. The extravert's gaze is directed outward. To him, at his most extraverted, the introvert may seem a bit of a creep. In fact, however, there is no such thing as a total introvert, or a total extravert. And one is not necessarily better off than the other; they are simply different. Naturally the extravert may prefer the company of other extraverts, while the introvert is usually happier among his own kind. This is akin to saying 'birds of a feather flock together', but there is no particular merit attached to either of the two psychological groupings.

Here is a set of questions designed to indicate to which group *you* belong. As likely as not you have a fair idea already. None the less, try the test and check up on yourself.

(1) Are you concerned that you should appear well dressed?

(2) If you saw an accident would you go at once to help?

(3) Do you regard thoughts about death as morbid?

(4) Do you think mysticism is rubbish?

(5) Would you rather talk than listen?

(6) Are you always prepared to compromise?

(7) Do you prefer to drink in company?

(8) Are you more interested in facts than theories?

(9) When you are wrong do you readily admit it?

(10) Do you like to work or play as one of a team?

(11) When you are angry do you make a scene?

(12) Do you admire confidence rather than caution?

(13) Are you a good mixer?

(14) Do you reach decisions quickly?

(15) Do you readily accept responsibility?

(16) Do you like to be one of a crowd at parties, etc.?

(17) Does being alone bore you?

(18) Are you able to shut your worries out of your mind?

(19) Do you feel at ease in public?

(20) Would you like to appear on television?

15

Each 'yes' gives one point towards extraversion, each 'no' is a point towards introversion. When the answer is 'yes and no' take a half mark on each side. If you find you have mostly 'yes' answers you are an extravert, whereas a preponderance of negatives suggests the label should be 'introvert'.

A fairly equal division, and particularly a high proportion of half marks, indicates a good balance. Now although neither grouping is superior to the other, it is plain enough that a reasonably-balanced personality has certain advantages. If from the test you find you are excessively introverted or extraverted, you'd be well advised to consider ways of reducing the sharpness of that inclination. You can't hope to change your basic type—and you might not want to—but you can control the more extreme manifestations in your personality.

First, let us consider the more obvious symptoms of the two groups. Ivor the introvert, if you should happen to see him at a cocktail party, will be close to a wall or in a quiet corner. He may be on his own or with someone as shy as himself and with whom he therefore finds common ground. He may be on the edge of a noisy group, half wishing he could be part of it, half afraid of forcing himself into a circle of (apparently extravert) people who find it so much easier to relax and, apparently, to enjoy themselves.

If Ivor were an alcoholic he would almost certainly drink alone. If he likes exercise—and the introvert doesn't have to be an indoor man—he will probably indulge in the more solitary or individual sports. The 'loneliness of the long-distance runner' will appeal to him more strongly than team sports. On a subject which holds his interest he may speak confidently, even brilliantly. Invited, however, to make an impromptu speech, he will run the risk of finding himself tongue-tied.

Ivor is not necessarily a rabbit. He may fly a jet fighter or be a competent surgeon or able scientist. On the other hand, he may be a dustman. According to some psychologists, he is more likely to be tall and thin than short and broad. But there is little convincing evidence of any direct relationship between physical character-istics and psychological groupings. The theory is akin to the assumption that fat people are happy and thin people miserable—which could be described as a load of old rubbish.

But that hale-and-hearty fellow over there, evidently the life and soul of the noisy group which Ivor would apparently like to join if he had the necessary bombast to shove his way in, that's Edgar the extravert. What do we know about *him*?

Edgar is in his element at a party. He's a talker more than a listener, and he talks well, catching the mood of his audience and carrying them along with him. When anyone else makes a joke, he's the first to laugh—even if he doesn't think it very funny. You can see from the way women react to him that he's used to easy conquests. Either way, he doesn't worry: a rebuff slides off him like water off a duck's back. He'll enter into an 'affair' lightly, and if anyone gets hurt it won't be him—he's in it for his pleasure; his emotions won't be involved at any depth. His enthusiasm is infectious. If he's a politician he's an opportunist, not an idealist as Ivor would be. If he's a businessman, he won't die poor. If one of the others in that group says something to annoy him, Edgar won't hide his anger: if the annoyance is sharp enough he'll fly into a rage, and he's not incapable of physical violence.

Ivor wouldn't react in that way at all. He'd turn

17

pale, and his fury would be silent, locked like poison in his brain. Edgar's anger on the other hand would be dissipated quickly in a blazing row. . . .

Neither of these two men has a balanced personality. But each, *if he wants to*, can do something to correct the imbalance.

The introvert can begin by taking up some extravert activity, something that will 'take him out of himself'. But if he truly loathes parties, why go? Punishing himself won't help. Better to find something more suitable to his temperament and which he is more likely to enjoy. It doesn't matter what it is, so long as his attention is diverted from himself.

He could gradually force himself into being less afraid of making a mistake, certainly one that is relatively unimportant. He should too, in these circumstances, admit his mistake and have the laugh against himself. That takes the sting out of embarrassment.

There is nothing to feel inferior about in being introverted. But if you feel you would like to be more extraverted, then push yourself whenever possible into extraverted company—and gradually you will find yourself less inhibited. You can listen to conversation, and express your opinion only when you feel you know what you're talking about—it's easier then.

The extravert can correct his imbalance by taking his eyes off the external realities which are uppermost in his thoughts, and forcing himself to indulge in a little introspection—perhaps a daily stint of self-examination. He may not enjoy it—quiet meditation will be less easy for him than it is for the introvert—but it's within his powers, and if he sticks to it he'll be doing himself a lot of good. If he finds his blustering 'hale fellow, well met' manner gets him into trouble—he should talk less and listen more. Giving others a chance to get into the limelight can work wonders and bring its own reward.

Stock-taking

Here are three basic questions you must ask yourself now; and ask yourself again when you've finished reading this book.

(1) What sort of person am I?
(2) With the awareness I now have of myself, which difficulties can I smooth out?
(3) How can I make the best use of the person I can then be?

Whatever conclusions you come to and whatever you see yourself to be, it's neither all good nor all bad. There are assets you can capitalize, abilities you can develop and put to good use. There are defects, too. Some you can put right; some you can't, and you must accept the situation and make the best of a bad job.

Once you know your handicaps you *can* attempt to overcome them. When a ship's captain knows his steering is defective, he'll give a wider berth to reefs and shoals than he might otherwise do. On the other hand the man who, for example, knows he can't take alcohol without blowing his top, should lay off the strong stuff. That's just common sense.

You are good at some things, poor at others. So, knowing what you can do and what you can't do—*set your sights accordingly.*

You know your capacity, capability. You know your limits, too. So why not plot your course and follow it with confidence—your personal, self-planned course? I'll give you the reason why you should: *once you truly know yourself, nothing can stop you!* Because you can drop pretences, accept realities, work with the tools you actually possess. Accept the limitations of your personal equipment, and the fact that some jobs call for tools which aren't in that kit. Who knows? You may acquire them later on, and then you can broaden your scope. Meanwhile, make full use of those tools—resources—which you do have at your command. . . . You must remember, however, that few of us truly and fully know ourselves; the rest of us can only get as near to it as possible.

The self-image

That broadly you should have the *right* picture of yourself and the *right* estimate of your potential is essential to your personal programme for purposeful living. To accept a completely *wrong* picture could be disastrous.

Let's look at some of the reasons why a realistic, honest self-appraisal is your first and most vital requirement.

Image and action trigger each other

You form your own self-image partly from your knowledge of what you can do, what you have done. Conversely, you will define what you can do in the future—what you want to do and what you intend to do—in terms of that established image. In other words, we 'act out' our own self-image. It follows that if you have an inadequate self-image you will aim short of your real potential, whereas if you have an exaggerated picture of yourself you will probably set yourself targets which will be unattainable.

In the first case you would be wasting your true potential. In the second, you would be heading for failure, frustration, and perhaps in the long run for psychiatric disorder.

Now however accurate and realistic our self-image may be, we must accept the fact that there will be occasions when (*a*) we will fail to live up to it, or (*b*) we will appear to surpass it. The reason for this is that while we regard ourselves as possessing one personality apiece, in fact each of us is several personalities compounded into one. Given one external stimulus, one 'personality' becomes involved: to a different stimulus, the reaction comes from another part of us. And so on . . . and not only different stimuli, but different circumstances play a part. So to ourselves, and to others who observe our varieties of behaviour, we seem 'unpredictable' or even 'contradictory'.

We must make allowances for these variable factors in our personalities. And having allowed that latitude, the fact remains that our thoughts, attitudes and actions are all influenced by our own self-image. The same thoughts and actions also influence and shape the image: so between image and performance there is a constant, two-way traffic.

In other words, when you feel good, don't you do better? Aren't you more confident, more 'outgoing', when you know you're looking good than when you're off-colour and have a spot on your chin?

Basic talents and abilities remain fundamentally the same. It is their expression, the use which is made of them, that can change dramatically in step with changes in self-image.

Self-knowledge=self-reliance

Self-consciousness—insecurity—feelings of personal inadequacy: these stem from lack of self-knowledge, from a confused or inaccurate self-image. When you have a realistic and clear self-image—which is the same as saying 'When you can look yourself in the face without embarrassment'—then you no longer worry about what other people think of you.

You no longer need their reassurance—because you no longer have those doubts about yourself.

It is from this position of self-reliance that you can afford to 'give' of your own personality. In other words, to relate positively to other people. Until you are sufficiently self-aware to be self-reliant, you feel dependent on the views and attitudes of other people. You are vulnerable—at the 'receiving end' of every relationship. The reverse of that situation is to direct your personality outwards, towards other people, instead of inwards at yourself and at *their* views of *you*: and you cannot do so until you recognize your own personality. In other words—I'm hammering the point deliberately —until you have built an accurate self-image.

The image will only be a true one if you accept reality. The mirror cannot lie, and in assessing your own personality you must be a true mirror to yourself. Remember there is no such thing as perfection—so it's a waste of time to hanker after it. If you have a long nose, all right, your nose is long. (It probably looks better on your kind of face than a short one would!) If you have an IQ of 110, don't pick a chess opponent who has one of 150.

Face facts—and accept them!

From self-knowledge to self-improvement

It is possible to compare the human mind to a magnetic tape or sound-track. Since birth, the tape has been recording sounds, messages, facts, beliefs, attitudes. These recordings, however jumbled, have been piling up since the moment of your birth. You aren't aware of them, but they comprise the material which has shaped your present views, attitudes and 'convictions'.

Deliberate and honest self-appraisal will reveal areas of thought where your inbuilt 'beliefs' (i.e. the recordings on the tape of your unconscious mind) conflict with facts which are now consciously known to you, and with the logical thought-processes of which you are now capable. So you'll recognize that a great deal of that tape's content is just hocus-pocus.

Armed with this knowledge, you can begin to clear the tape . . .

Target selection through self-knowledge

Establishing the self-image is necessary not only to decide how far we can go in a given direction, how high we can set our sights; it is necessary in order to select the direction, the area in which we can most effectively operate.

Whoever you are, whatever sort of person you are, there are fields in which you can be successful and others in which you can be only a dunce. To *be yourself* you must deliberately select the area in which you can *fulfil yourself*; and you can't do that until you *know yourself*.

Using the brain-computer

Each of us has certain inborn capabilities—physical and mental. But it's no use having the build of a heavyweight champion if you never learn to co-ordinate your movements: similarly it's useless having the brain of an Einstein if you don't know how to use it.

The human brain can be compared to a highly sophisticated computer. Like a computer, it has to be fed with data before it can churn out an answer. And data is useless, of course, unless it's accurate. So how can you expect your brain-computer to give you the right answer to any problem which concerns you if you fail to give it complete and accurate information about yourself?

If your self-image is unrealistic you will have fed in wrong data and you'll get a wrong answer.

So it boils down to this: *you cannot live purposefully, effectively, without a reasonably accurate self-image*.

When you have made this vital personal assessment you will feel enormous relief—like a huge weight lifting from your shoulders. No longer need you waste your life and suffer the strain of trying to be what you've always thought or been told you *ought* to be. Recognizing yourself, now you can *be* yourself.

You are *you*. You always have been.

Now, by accepting the reality of yourself—as Cromwell said, 'warts and all'—*you will become twice the man you were!*

Be your own analyst

You won't discover what sort of person you are simply by thinking about it for a minute and then grabbing at a few quick answers. And even when you've made a thorough estimation, you can't just leave it at that and Rest In Peace. Because people change: *you* change. You aren't exactly the person you were last year—and in six months there'll be new changes.

To possess an accurate and up-to-date self-image, you must check, evaluate and revaluate constantly. Experience teaches you about yourself—but you have to *think* about it if you want to learn its lessons.

To set *you* thinking about *yourself*, I shall be giving sets of questions throughout this book. There will be no answers; you must come to conclusions for yourself.

24

The questions are to *stimulate you into habits of self-analysis*.

If you answer these questions honestly—or with a reasonable degree of honesty—they tell you something about yourself. Whatever the lesson may be, you will find some parallel, and suggestions relating to it, in the main text of the book. Make a written note of the weaknesses you discover: and a note of the page numbers which can help you. This will give you an easy reference when you come to re-read that section.

And now here's a method of using these questions to build *and improve* your own self-image:

(1) Answer each set of questions as honestly as you can.

(2) Write brief, clear notes of your answers. Think hard about the kind of personality which is revealed by these indications.

(3) Imagine in your mind's eye a person who corresponds to the resultant image. Rather like constructing one of those police 'Identikit' pictures!

(4) If you've been really honest, some aspects of the picture won't much appeal to you—even though you know it's a portrait of yourself! Well, don't shy away: look more closely. Analyse what's wrong. Concentrate on what you can do to change the picture—*by changing the reality behind it!*

CHAPTER THREE

SOMEBODY SOMEWHERE HATES YOUR GUTS

Does the thought chill you? Does it make you want to hide? Or perhaps your reaction is one of resentment so that you bluster angrily 'Well, I hate *him*, too!'

If you react in any of those ways, you're way off beam. After all, do you love everyone *you* meet?

Of course you don't—not unless you're some kind of angel. And if you think about it, you'll realize that to expect to be liked by everyone is absurd. It is also absurd, then, to resent the fact that X or Y has apparently taken a dislike to you.

Now if the opening sections of this book have given any illumination at all, they will have thrown light on two closely related areas. First, you will have begun to understand yourself a little better. Second, you will have begun to appreciate that there are many ways in which people's temperaments and personalities vary. People are individuals, each different—*different*, not superior or inferior.

I am not addressing myself to any single individual or to any particular *type* of individual. This book is intended for you and the man next door and the woman down the road; it's intended for the bus conductor and the managing director, and if the Archbishop of Canterbury wants to read it that's fine. The fact that your views and attitudes differ from your neighbour's doesn't mean one is right and the other wrong. You're different, that's all.

So you've just realized that Jones dislikes you. Do you think it might help if you pick a fight with him next time you meet? Or nurse the grievance of his disliking you? Perhaps your way out would be to tell your friends and acquaintances what a so-and-so that fellow Jones is?

I would like to persuade you to take a slightly more mature view of the situation.

First of all, you aren't perfect. No one is. If you can admit to yourself that you do have a fault or two, wouldn't you credit Jones with the ability to spot some of them? All right, so how is that *his* business. . . . But we all have our sensitive spots, and those weaknesses or characteristics of yours could be the very traits which Jones dislikes. They might not be faults at all—they could be mannerisms, or simply the way you *appear* to him. And how about your feelings towards Jones—apart from the fact (or impression) that he doesn't seem to take to you with much enthusiasm, isn't it just possible that *you* started the mutual antipathy by appearing not to like the look or sound of *him*?

He could be shy and lacking in self-confidence —afraid to be natural—and so appear uninterested, even rude. If you react to this with indifference, perhaps with ill-concealed aggression, you're hardly likely to become friends!

Cast your mind back. Likes and dislikes are nearly always mutual and reciprocal.

If on reflection you see you might have been at fault, the remedy is in your hands. But there's another possibility: could it be that Jones has an 'unfortunate manner', an *appearance* of unfriendliness, which you mistook for personal antagonism?

27

That can happen, particularly with the 'shy' or introverted character. As I have suggested, he may be too shy to smile, too hesitant to reciprocate normally when he's offered the hand of friendship.

The one thing he doesn't need is your dislike. What he *does* need is your understanding.

(*a*) The *basis* of your attempt to understand him will be your own self-awareness. You must know something about yourself before you can establish effective relationships.

(*b*) The *motive* will be your desire to relate to others. It is as much in your own interests as in theirs that you should do so, and the first step is to understand them.

(*c*) The *means* can be covered in a single, all-important word—*communication*.

Communication

The art of living is the art of handling personal relationships. The ability to communicate—to understand and be understood—is the bridge between people which makes such relationships possible.

There are some who find communication so difficult that they give up altogether. Often this kind of person buys a dog. A dog tends to devote itself to its owner, and the owner encourages this by training the animal to obey and love him. The sort of person I'm talking about finds a great advantage in this kind of relationship over any other, through the dog's relative inability to disagree or answer back.

The man I am describing is the fellow who replaces human contacts with animal ones—and you might be surprised how often it happens. This serves to illustrate a point: that communicating isn't all that easy. It calls for thought, application and constant practice, and not all of us have the capacity for those things or the persistence to develop them.

Let's return now to Jones, the man who doesn't like you. Ask yourself.

(1) *What's wrong with me as he sees me?*
(2) *Is it a fault I can do something to correct?*

If the answer is 'yes, it is', you've already profited from the experience of being disliked. Through someone's reaction to you, you have learnt something about yourself. But if there is no positive answer to those questions, try this one:

(3) *What is it in Jones's temperament that makes him dislike me?*

Try to understand his point of view: see yourself through his 'window'. To do that, you must get to know him. In other words, you must reply to his negative attitude with a positive one. The process is illustrated on page 30.

The bottom line establishes the beginnings of what may become a rewarding human relationship. You will, moreover, find that you have a deep sense of satisfaction in having transformed a negative situation into a positive one. Jones, you see, needs help as much as you do: Jones may in truth be 'you', and 'you' may be the character I've described as Jones. Each needs the understanding of the other and the ability to communicate with the other. Without the initiative which in the diagram below has been shown by 'you', our picture would be much simpler: all we'd need to draw would be a pair of dogs snarling at each other, hackles raised . . .

We humans were born for better things than that. But we have to work at it. No man on earth is 100 per cent mature, any more than you could find one totally immature. In all of us there are gaps to be bridged, cracks to be filled in. Knowing your own weaknesses,

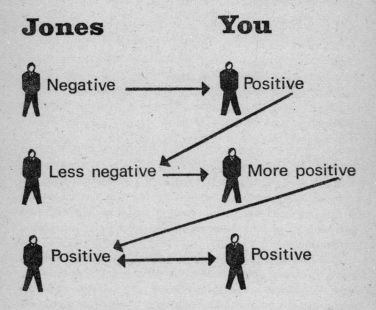

Jones   **You**

Negative ⟶ Positive

Less negative ⟶ More positive

Positive ⟷ Positive

you can understand and tolerate other people's. It certainly isn't a one-way traffic: each will be making the most of the other.

Two-way understanding

Now think back for a moment to that question of not setting your targets beyond your capacity. Wouldn't it be just as pointless to expect more of another person than he is capable of producing? If, for example, a man's educational and home background has limited his vocabulary to a dozen four-letter words, you wouldn't expect him to understand the works of Jean-Paul Sartre, would you?

Put as simply as that, it sounds obvious. But how often do parents and their children fail to understand each other because they (the parents) expect their children to think or react like adults?

A child has a child's mentality; an adolescent is called adolescent because he is not yet adult. If you expect either of them to see things as you do, you are asking the impossible and you will fail to establish a realistic basis for communication. Each may walk off shrugging, angry, muttering 'Oh, what's the *use* . . .'

We will be discussing adult/child relationships in chapter 18. Returning now to the purely adult area, I'd like to give you an example of the enormous difference which a friendly, flexible attitude—as opposed to a rigid, antagonistic one which can only result in mutual hostility—can make.

Soon after World War II ended in the Far East, Lord Louis Mountbatten was Commander-in-Chief in Singapore. He had personal responsibility for vast areas of South-East Asia, huge territories in which the power-vacuum following Japan's defeat presented enormous, even terrifying problems in both human and political terms. Mountbatten the brilliant war leader was now Mountbatten the hard-pressed civil administrator, and few men in history can have faced greater problems.

Most of the troops on whom Lord Mountbatten relied for maintenance of peace and order were from India. Now Pandit Nehru, soon to become India's Prime Minister, was about to visit Singapore. There were discontented elements among the Indian fraternity,

31

and one of Nehru's intentions was to lay a wreath on a memorial to Indian soldiers who had lost their lives fighting as allies of the Japanese. The situation was potentially explosive, and if Nehru's visit had the effect which many feared it might have, disaster loomed ahead.

Mountbatten, returning to Singapore from a tour of other territories, found that in his absence plans had been drawn up to restrict the visitor's movements, limit his contacts with the Indian community: in effect, to treat him as an unwelcome and dangerous guest.

One can imagine what adverse effects might have resulted.

Lord Louis immediately cancelled all such arrangements. He met Pandit Nehru as a friend instead of as an enemy. He gave him his own official car, and unrestricted access to everything and everyone the Indian leader wished to see. Lord and Lady Mountbatten entertained their visitor royally. The two men drove together through the teeming crowds—and the crowds saw them not as enemies, but friends. Nehru abandoned his plan to lay that wreath.

One man's insight and common sense averted what might have been an ugly situation. Indeed the effect went much further. It established a deep and sincere personal friendship which in the years to come contributed very largely to Anglo-Indian relations and to peace on the Indian sub-continent. And let's not forget that *two* men share the credit—Mountbatten for extending the hand of friendship, and Nehru for accepting it with equal intelligence and warmth.

We can't all be Commanders-in-Chief or Prime Ministers. Your influence and mine may extend only to an infinitely small circle of people. But the lesson is the same, and so are the effects.

Somewhere around the end of the last century, the American Elbert Hubbard wrote:

Because you do not like a man is no reason he is your enemy: this is a busy world, and none of us have time to sit down and hate one another. The only enemies we have are those we conjure forth from our own inner consciousness. The idea that a man has enemies is, after all, only egotism gone to seed.

You are what you are and what you make of yourself. Equally, you must accept that your fellow man is *himself*. Neither is superior to the other: you are simply *different*.

And *vive la différence*!

CHAPTER FOUR

YOU AND YOUR IQ

'IQ' stands for Intelligence Quotient, and it is a measurement of capacity to learn.

Fortunately, we are all interested in ourselves. I say fortunately, because this makes it more likely that you will want to *know yourself* and *know about yourself*. And among the things which many people would like to know about themselves is the answer to 'What is my IQ?'

In other words, to 'How intelligent am I?'

It's because of this—because intelligence is one of the ingredients of your personality—that I am including this short chapter. But at the risk of infuriating you, I must make it clear that I am *not* going to provide you with an answer to that question. For two good reasons:

(1) It would need a whole book, not just a chapter, to tell you how to measure your IQ.
(2) In terms of the purpose of this book, it doesn't matter *what* your IQ may be!

In other words, *I don't care how clever you are*. Now I'll try to explain why.

Intelligence

We ought to start with a definition: what *is* intelligence?

For our purpose here, let's settle for calling it *the capacity for judgement, comprehension and reasoning, and the ability to relate this capacity to constructive purposes.*

The IQ gives an index-figure which gauges this capacity. It is a code-grouping arrived at through the subject performing practical tests: it is not therefore, of scientific exactitude.

The development of this intelligence-rating scale was initiated in France in 1904 by a Frenchman called Binet. His first study was of mentally subnormal children; then he went on to establish groupings of 'mental age'. By evolving a set of problems normally solvable by five-year-olds, for instance, he was able to say that a child of four who could pass that test (but not the next one up the scale) had a 'mental age of five'—or, 'one year advanced'. But 'one year advanced' was of no use as a measurement, because to be a year ahead at four shows a greater relative precocity than it does to be one year advanced at fourteen. What was needed was the *ratio* of advancement or retardment; and this was the concept from which the IQ scale was developed.

As a rough guide to IQ ratings throughout the population, we can say that about half would score between 90 and 110, a quarter would do better than that, and the other quarter worse. Only one-half of one per cent of the population have IQ's above 140; whereas to get a middling university degree demands a rating of about 125.

An interesting phenomenon is that parents with high IQ's tend to produce children with a slightly lower IQ than their own, whereas parents with IQ's below 90 can expect their children to check-out a few points higher up the scale. (This is fortunate as otherwise the range of human intelligence would diverge progressively into brilliance on one hand and idiocy on the other.

Eventually we'd all be either geniuses or mad, and the difference between the two might not be all that evident!)

Of course if your IQ is below average certain careers will be closed to you because you will be unable to pass the necessary examinations. Conversely, if you have an exceptionally high IQ you'll be wasting your potential if you take a job as a road-sweeper. But the great point is—that no matter what your IQ—if you live your life to the full of your capacity you will have little to grumble about.

Potential

This word is the key. Your IQ shows your *potential*. It is an indication of what you *could* achieve if you made full use of that potential. But there is a difference between *potential* and *performance*.

You could have an IQ of 150 and be too lazy to make use of it. You could have one of 140 and be so personally obnoxious to your fellow men (for instance, incapable of handling personal relationships effectively) that you're impossible to work with. There are a thousand ways in which you can fail to realize your potential—a popular method is to deaden the mind with alcohol.

What matters most is *how to use what you've got*. There are millions of highly successful men and women who wouldn't qualify for high IQ ratings. And just as many top-notch IQ-rated citizens are singularly unsuccessful people. They are often unhappy too—neuroses of all kinds romp with extraordinary abandon among the higher orders of intelligence.

I'm not saying that if you have a high IQ you must be a neurotic. Of course not. What I *am* saying is that your IQ is not generally a significant factor in your success or failure as a human being.

(I suppose I should qualify that statement. Some textbooks group people with IQ's below 70 as 'feeble-minded'. Further categorizations are:

> from 70 down to 50, morons
> from 50 down to 25, imbeciles
> from 25 downwards, idiots.

Naturally people in these groups cannot live full lives; they are limited. But these are the extreme cases, the unfortunate exceptions.)

If your IQ is 100—which is the average for the population as a whole—and you *use your full potential*, you will win hands-down over someone whose rating is 120 who hasn't learnt (or can't be bothered) to make use of his capabilities.

A little knowledge is dangerous. That's an old saying —and it's true, because the lower your IQ the more you may imagine that *knowing a little* about a subject turns you into an expert on it. Whereas in fact it should make you realize that *there is much more to know*.

For instance, in this chapter I've tried to explain briefly what Intelligent Quotients are, what their purpose is and how important (or *un*important) *your* IQ is as an element in your personality. But the outline which you've read here certainly won't make you an expert on the subject!

Knowledge

This isn't always necessary to us. I mean the acquired knowledge, facts and figures absorbed through deliberrate study of a subject. Practical experience can teach you more than many a university course. And intuition can span the gaps and barriers of years of learning.

The important thing is to use what capacity you have. To develop and use your potential to its maximum effect. Just because you're not an intellectual whiz-kid is no reason to regard yourself as an also-ran. *If your IQ is below average, don't waste time and energy worrying about it. Use every ounce, every milligram, of what you've got.*

CHAPTER FIVE

YOU AREN'T THE ONLY PEBBLE ON THE BEACH

No—but you're one of them. One of millions, each of which, remember, is shaped by its contacts with the others. . . .

I said right from the start that if you're going to get any satisfaction out of life, people have got to *like* you. At first glance, this may seem to conflict with something I said later—namely that to expect to be liked by everyone is absurd.

In fact there is no contradiction. Putting it simply: not everyone is going to like you, but if you handle your relationships to the best advantage you will make more friends and fewer adversaries than if you left the whole thing to chance.

Human communication

Human relationships play too vital a part in the business of living to be treated casually. If you are going to get the most out of life, it will demand your time, thought and conscious effort. (In time, the effort will become so natural to you that it will be to a large extent unconscious. Practice makes perfect—but practice also makes it easy.) Relating to other people is basic to every field of human activity, and it requires not merely bursts of concentrated effort on particular occasions but continuous, life-long study and application.

Treating people as people must be a way of life, not a tool to be switched on and off according to mood, impulse or situation. The salesman whose winning smile fades as soon as he has clinched (or failed to clinch) the deal is not a salesman—he's a phoney.

But there's nothing phoney about trying to make people like you. It's not dishonest or hypocritical either. Whether the relationship is social or commercial, the honest intention to make the most and best of it, to evoke confidence and good will, entirely justifies the deliberate use of skills and techniques directed solely to that end.

Any fool can get the worst out of people. There are hundreds of ways of rubbing a man up the wrong way, treating him casually or rudely. If you want to go the whole hog, you can spit in his eye and jump on his toes. To achieve the opposite effect—to make him feel *good*—requires rather more effort and considerably more intelligence. There is no merit in being outspoken unless you are very sure of yourself. In being blunt you must be careful not to offend.

Now I'm assuming you are reasonably intelligent. That's the least you would expect. In any dialogue don't you prefer the other man to treat you as an adult, intelligent person?

Of course you do. So do I. We are all flattered when our views are sought, when we are allowed to feel that our opinions matter as much as, if not more than, the other person's. We like our talents to be recognized, and we prefer people who, when we meet them, discuss subjects in which they know we are interested. On the other side of the coin, we have our weaknesses, areas where we're not as well informed as we might be, and so on, and we

How to encourage your child to read with STORYCHAIR and CAROUSEL BOOKS- a free offer.

Your child needs to read. **STORYCHAIR** and **CAROUSEL BOOKS** are selected by Anne Wood, a mother who is Chairman of the **Federation of Children's Book Groups** for parents.

Her advice to parents, and extracts from these beautiful books, appear in **Children's Reading: A Parents Guide.**

For your FREE copy, fill in your address below and mail this card.

Please send me my free copy of Children's Reading: A Parents Guide.

Name

Address

10

2

BUSINESS REPLY SERVICE
LICENCE No. NW 1067

TRANSWORLD PUBLISHERS LIMITED
Department C
CAVENDISH HOUSE
57/59 UXBRIDGE ROAD
LONDON W5 4BR

don't look forward to a second meeting with the acquaintance who draws attention to them.

We're human, that's all . . .

Do unto others as you would they should do unto you. Throughout history—dating back certainly as far as 1600 B.C.—this very simple thought has been expressed countless times by thinkers, writers, prophets and philosophers. Putting the same precept into the context of this book—

If you want people to treat you as being worthy of respect, treat them the same way.

How, when and where?

How? in every way that's open to you. I shall be describing some of these in the following chapters.

When? every minute of your waking life.

Where? everywhere!

This book is a simple blueprint for everyone, and the precepts in it are applicable in all situations and walks of life. If you are reading this at home, why not start practising right *now*, within your own four walls?

And having discussed the subject in general terms, it's time to get down to cases. To examples of circumstances under which *you*, by treating people as people, can not only benefit them but also earn enormous dividends for yourself.

But wait just one minute . . .

You will find that from time to time I shall repeat myself. This is quite deliberate. First, to drive home the points already covered, reinforcing them by repetition, for it is essential that you should keep them alive and fresh in your mind. Second, because I am sketching out a whole pattern for purposeful relationships between people, and as piece after piece is fitted into the jigsaw we need to look back at what we've done, to see the picture as it develops. So now, let me summarize the main issues so far discussed.

KNOW YOURSELF—your powers and your limitations. You can then:

(1) Establish attainable and worthwhile goals for yourself.
(2) By recognizing areas of weakness, try to correct them.
(3) Through understanding your own personality, begin to understand others.

RECOGNIZE THE OTHER PERSON'S RIGHT TO BE DIFFERENT—without imagining that such differences imply that one is better than the other. Use the opportunity to learn more about yourself from the way others react to you.

MAKE THE MOST OF EVERY HUMAN CONTACT. Start with the positive intention of making your relationship a fruitful one. To start with a chip on your shoulder is like trying to swim with your boots on!

Be yourself. Allow the other man the privilege of being himself. See his point of view as well as your own. Behave to him as you would like him to behave to you.

That's the strategy. Let's look and see how it can be applied in differing situations.

Be Your Own Analyst: 1

How Much Have You Learnt from Your Own Experience?

To assess whether or not you have profited from your personal experiences in life and to have some idea of your own performance and potential, answer YES or NO to whether you can give IMMEDIATE answers to each of the following questions:

(1) *What accomplishment are you most proud of?*
(2) *Which aspect of your personality is most pleasing to you?*
(3) *What incident in your memory are you most ashamed of?*
(4) *If you could re-live any five years of your life, which would you choose?*
(5) *If you could change one aspect of your character, which would it be?*

You are not required to give the answers—only to answer YES or NO to whether you are able to answer the question without having to think it out. If you need time to think, the answer to that question must be NO.

CHAPTER SIX

NOBODY WINS AN ARGUMENT

Who wins most? (*a*) The man who pulverizes his opponent's theory, destroys his beliefs and leaves him helplessly defeated, or (*b*) the debater who puts his own point of view, gives due consideration to his opponent's, and perhaps in the final outcome 'agrees to differ'?

Well, the first man has certainly made sure everyone knows he's won the contest. He's shown it as conclusively as if he'd knocked the fellow down and then jumped on his prone body. But hasn't he lost at least as much as he's won—by making an enemy?

That's an odd kind of victory—the way a bulldozer wins its arguments. He's scored, he's triumphed. Perhaps that's what he set out to do, and now he can strut away filled with satisfaction.

If that's the case, he hasn't travelled far from the playground of his nursery school.

The most important things in life are people. 'Getting on' with people, liking them, having them like you. Demonstrating your 'superiority' isn't much of a contribution in *that* department. So why do it?

I'm not suggesting you become a 'yes man', agree to things you know to be wrong or keep your opinions to yourself in case someone else might find them objectionable. I'm not saying you shouldn't indulge in arguments.

What I *am* saying is that the man who puts his case, allows the other fellow to put his and listens to it, can win his argument just as completely *and not make an enemy in the process.*

Making enemies—losing friends, missing the opportunity to make a friend—any fool can do that. You don't have to try, or work at it: just let things slide, and it'll be happening all the time. To achieve the opposite, though—well, this calls for the intelligence and reasoning-power which distinguishes the human from the beast.

One of my friends who spent the war in uniform gave me a definition of what in his experience constituted an 'argument' in a Service mess. It had four stages, I remember, each leading directly to the next:

   (i) Statement of fact
  (ii) Direct contradiction
 (iii) Personal abuse
 (iv) Physical assault

That definition is intended to be funny, of course. But if we allow for exaggeration (and a dram or two of alcohol in the participants) it may not be so wide of the mark. War is the antithesis of civilized behaviour, and it gives rise to crudities in human relationships. At certain levels, it may have a stultifying effect on a man's intellect. But not on all: and I can get back to my point by recalling that it was the Duke of Wellington who said: 'Nothing except a battle lost can be half so melancholy as a battle won' . . .

I'm not suggesting that anyone should want to lose an argument. If facts and logic are on your side, you ought to prove your point. But, for heaven's sake, win gracefully! Win without symbolically kicking your adversary in the teeth, and you'll have won not only the argument but also respect, approval, friendship.

Isn't that a *real* victory?

If you win gracefully, your opponent can lose without 'losing face'. Instead of disliking you for making him look silly, he will give you credit for your knowledge and ability. Although one set of opinions will have triumphed over another, each man will have heard and discussed the other's point of view. Such an exchange will become in retrospect an exercise in communication which will bring you closer together. You will have achieved something positive instead of something futile.

The importance of diplomacy

There is an ancient and well-used principle in diplomacy which bears closely on this subject. It is that you must always leave your opponent room for manoeuvre, room to side-step and 'save face'. It's no more than common sense, is it? If you push a man into a corner from which he has no escape route, his only way out is by attacking you.

The purpose of diplomacy is to avoid wars, not to make them inevitable. In human relationships the same principle can be—*must be* applied.

Here is one way of 'winning':

'So there you are, see? Proved it, haven't I? Ought to get our facts right, mate, before you start telling me what's what. I know what I'm talking about—you ought to think twice before you get arguing about things you don't understand—'

And here's another:

'Yes—well, I can see what you meant. It's a way of looking

46

at it, certainly, and you're partly right, except that—' (chuckle)
*'Anyway, we're really saying the same thing, in different
ways . . .'*

Very likely they weren't saying the same thing at all.
The last speaker has proved his point quite clearly,
and even though he knows his opponent was talking
arrant rubbish he's ready to let him down lightly. He
has the sense to know you can win an argument without putting the boot in too.

Of course if you're on the losing side of the argument
and you know you're in the wrong, it is best to admit it
and give way gracefully. This disarms your opponent
who will appreciate your honesty and be forced to
admire you.

Simple? Obvious? Well, perhaps it is. But so are
most things that are worth remembering. And next
time you get heated in an argument, pause and cast
your mind back to these simple truths. If you find you're
getting worked up, that's the moment to keep quiet for
a bit while you cool off. You may realize, on reflection,
that the things we've been talking about are so 'obvious'
that in the heat of argument and anxiety to 'win' you've
ignored the obvious altogether.

If you come to *that* conclusion, reflect a little more;
try to estimate how many times it's happened. Whatever
the figure, that's the number of friends you've lost.

Another tip—to be remembered when you're arguing and you feel the pressure rising. I've said 'keep
quiet for a bit while you cool off'—but you can do
better than that. *Break into the argument—cool it, yourself and your opponent by pleading guilty to possessing strong
feelings on this particular subject. Tell him it's something you
feel deeply about so that in discussing it you're tempted to 'blow
your top' . . .*

After that, it's less likely that you *will* get over-heated:

and if you do, at least your adversary can understand and accept your virulence with a smile!

Logic

While we're discussing the art of argument, let me put in a plea for one ingredient which seems all too often to be forgotten or ignored . . .

That little thing called *logic*!

Half the time we spend arguing with each other nowadays we aren't arguing about facts at all, but about figments of our own imagination! In other words we are being emotionally motivated.

Many are so anxious to hate or rebel against something that when it isn't there they invent it!

Small wonder a great deal of heat is engendered, passions inflamed and even friendships broken, simply because of an imaginary enemy or evil which doesn't exist. Reason flies out of the window and those involved behave as if they were in a drunken brawl. It is difficult to be objective if we allow ourselves to be victims of our subjective feelings, and it isn't always easy to sort out our own emotions and prejudices. But we can make a strong and conscious effort to try.

You want examples?

In chapter 4, I pointed out that your IQ measurement is only a gauge of your potential. It's no good having the fastest horse in the race if you're not a good enough jockey to get him out from behind the others so that he can use his speed. But if you read that chapter carelessly you might think I suggested that half-witted people are more useful than clever ones.

In fact I said nothing of the sort. But I can imagine a not-untypical television discussion in which it could take some minutes to persuade my opponent that I didn't.

A very common example of the same phenomenon is that of *reaction to emotive words* . . .

For instance, 'patriotism' is sometimes regarded as being synonymous with 'aggressive nationalism'. Conversely, a youth with long hair is often assumed to be an habitual fornicator and drug-addict with anarchic leanings.

So hostility is engendered without justifiable reason. It doesn't stop there, either, because arguments motivated by non-logical inspiration tend to follow a vicious circle:

(i)   The row becomes more and more heated;
(ii) Heat—temper—tends further to reduce your powers of reasoning;
(iii) Eventually it's a shouting-match—about as dignified and constructive as two cats spitting at each other.

Can there be anything more ludicrous than losing your temper over something which exists only in your imagination? There isn't. So before you open fire—*make sure your target isn't just a mirage*.

Friends don't grow on trees, and you can't afford to lose any. The Duc de la Rochefoucauld, who peppered the seventeenth century with a great deal of horse sense, wrote this:

He who thinks he can find in himself the means of doing without others is much mistaken: but he who thinks that others cannot do without him is still more mistaken.

So remember—
Don't try to win an argument if winning means losing a friend. In the long run you'd do better to lose—and win one!

49

(1) *Do you react to disappointment by* (a) sulking; (b) working out what went wrong and planning to correct it next time; (c) blaming the others ininvolved; (d) pretending you don't give a damn anyway?

(2) *Faced with challenge, do you* (a) grasp it; (b) find a way to avoid confrontation; (c) pretend not to have noticed it?

(3) *When your instincts tell you to take a certain action, do you* (a) do it immediately; (b) ask advice, and then act; (c) decide to sleep on it?

(4) *When you're depressed, over-tired, do you* (a) force yourself to go on working; (b) knock off until you feel more up to it?

(5) *When you don't get on well with a colleague at work, do you* (a) avoid him as much as possible; (b) have frequent rows with him; (c) seek ways or opportunities to improve the relationship?

(6) *When someone deliberately acts against you, do you* (a) nurse the grudge; (b) seek revenge; (c) try to ignore what's happened; (d) have it out with him face to face?

(7) *When you meet someone who's more successful than yourself, are you* (a) jealous and resentful; (b) subservient, obsequious; (c) frankly interested in discovering the secret of his success?

(8) *When you feel a bad mood coming on, do you* (a) surrender to it; (b) try to keep yourself to yourself until it passes; (c) snap yourself out of it?

(9) *Faced with a new proposal which would entail some drastic changes, do you* (a) search for reasons to reject it; (b) consider the pros and cons objectively; (c) ignore it altogether?

(10) *When you hear that someone has expressed an adverse opinion of you, do you* (a) think about what was said and consider whether there could be truth in it; (b) take no notice; (c) set counter-rumours going about the person who said it; (d) go straight along and tax him with it?

CHAPTER SEVEN

NOW LOOK HERE, YOU!

Now a few critical comments on the subject of criticism. Let's start with a piece of film about an office drama. We're in rehearsal, and we're going to run the shot in two different ways.

The scene is an office. Backstage is a large 'executive-type' desk cluttered with telephones, papers, etc. This desk is unoccupied at present. Against the side wall, however, is a smaller one at which an attractive SECRETARY is pounding a typewriter. The speed at which she is working, and the mounting pile of typed pages, indicates that she is certainly earning her weekly pay-packet. The clock on the wall informs us that it is 3.30 p.m. As the secretary changes another page in her machine, the door opens and her BOSS hurries in. He looks as if he's had a good lunch on his expense account.

BOSS (*slumping into his chair behind his desk*): How's that report coming along?

SECRETARY: Won't be long now. I told Mr. Johnson we'd have it done by four o'clock, and——

BOSS: You *what*?

SECRETARY: He sent Angela along. Apparently the Board's in a hurry for it. So I told her to tell him——

BOSS (*glaring, red in the face*): Who told you you could tell him anything of the sort?

SECRETARY: I'm afraid I don't understand. It *will* be ready by four o'clock——

BOSS: But that's only a *draft*! There'll be dozens of things to change before I can let the Chairman see it! Oh, my God!

SECRETARY: I'm sorry. If I'd known it was only a draft——

BOSS (*jumping to his feet*): You should know better than to send messages to the Managing Director without my approval. Now I've got to go and see him, and explain it won't be ready, then he'll have to explain it to the Chairman, and—*damn and blast*!

SECRETARY: I'm *extremely* sorry. If I'd thought——

BOSS: That's half the trouble—you *don't* think (*moving towards the door, furious*) Miss Smith. Your lack of thought has caused a great deal of trouble and a waste of several senior executives' valuable time. Now if you want to keep your job here, you'd better realize once and for all that I will not tolerate . . .

Cut! And now let's shoot it again with new dialogue.

Everything is exactly the same up to the moment of the BOSS's entrance.

BOSS: How's that report coming along?

SECRETARY: Won't be long now. I told Mr. Johnson we'd have it done by four o'clock and——

BOSS: You did what?

SECRETARY: He sent Angela along. Apparently the Board's in a hurry for it. So I told her to tell him——

BOSS (*gazing at her in consternation*): Oh, Lord . . .

SECRETARY: Shouldn't I have?

BOSS: No you shouldn't . . . Damn it, I should have told you. That's not the final version, you see—it's only a draft. There'll be quite a lot of changes before it's ready to be seen.

SECRETARY: I'm terribly sorry. I should have re-alized——

BOSS: It's my fault for not warning you ... Well, I'd better go and straighten this out.

SECRETARY: Would you like me to go and——

BOSS (*standing up*): No. I'll fix it. But look, *next* time——

SECRETARY: I know. *Next* time, I'll keep quiet.

BOSS (*en route for the door*): If you do, you'll be the first woman that ever did!

He needn't wory. She *will*, next time ... But you see the difference, don't you? In neither case will the secretary repeat her mistake: the lesson's learnt. In case two, the boss won't make *his* mistake again either. He comes out best, though, because he has a competent, pleasant secretary. And she's likely to stay with him whereas the betting is that the man in shot one will be looking for a new girl within a matter of days.

Moral: there are times when you have to criticize, but you must know *how*. In one word, criticism must be *constructive*.

Edmund Burke, an Irishman of the eighteenth century, wrote:

Is it in destroying and pulling down that skill is displayed? The shallowest understanding, the rudest hand, is more than equal to that task!

(i) The only legitimate aim of criticism is to correct, improve or instruct the person who is being criticized. If the criticism isn't likely to achieve that, it's far better not voiced.

(ii) Unless you *have* to criticize—don't.

(iii) If you feel you have to—well, wait a bit, think about it, work out what it will or won't achieve.

54

(iv) If the answer is 'nothing' or 'not much', drop it. If it will achieve something worthwhile, go ahead. But—

(v) Give thought to your choice of words. Anyone can accept criticism if it's so worded that they feel it stems from friendship, love, the urge to help. Whereas—

(vi) Nobody willingly accepts criticism which is an expression of aggression. Instead of opening with 'You idiot, why on earth did you do such a stupid thing?', wrap up what you want to say so that it sounds more like good advice. Gambits such as:

'I wonder how it would have turned out if you'd done it *this* way instead . . .'

'Has it struck you, I wonder, if you'd taken *that* course you might have got better results?'

'Well, I dare say I'd have done exactly as you did. But—hindsight is easy, of course—maybe it would have worked out better if you'd . . .'

Perhaps some of these openings sound a bit 'smarmy'. I'm not trying to feed it to you word for word—there are no lines you need learn by heart. I'm only trying to suggest some ways in which that otherwise bitter pill of criticism can be sugar-coated to make it palatable.

Some years ago, I learned a valuable lesson from a village policeman. It happened because I'd done a stupid thing while driving my car—but the lesson was more in human relationships and the art of criticism than in good behaviour on the road.

I had a problem on my mind that morning, and was so preoccupied that I turned right-handed into a side road without paying proper attention to the oncoming traffic. The squeal of another car's brakes and the blaring of its horn awakened me to the fact that I had given no hand signal and left barely enough room to avert a serious accident. At about the same moment I noticed a policeman on a motor-cycle: he'd seen what had happened, turned behind me and swept past and ahead of my car, ordering me to stop.

I was more shocked at realizing how crassly I'd behaved than that I had been caught. As I stopped the car, my hands were trembling. I knew that in the last few seconds there might easily have been a fatal accident.

The policeman left his bike standing right in front of my car, and walked slowly, sternly to the driving-seat window. I was searching my brain for an excuse, some way to shed the blame. But he gave me no chance to speak.

'You know, it's a funny thing, sir,' he said. 'Makes no odds how long a man's been driving or how good a driver he is, he can still do a bloody silly thing now and then . . .'

I looked at him in amazement. I was even more amazed to see a smile on his face.

I've often thought about that policeman. I hope he's a Chief Superintendent by now—he ought to be at least that. For he knew a great deal more than mere traffic laws: he knew how to deal with people.

I doubt if I've done anything so silly on the road since that day. And often, when I read of someone being fined or imprisoned for a motoring offence, I think to myself, If only he'd had the luck to meet *my* policeman on some earlier occasion!

Criticism and tact

Of course criticism is necessary sometimes. The lesson to learn is how to offer it in a manner which won't produce the opposite effect of that intended. Your object, after all, is to improve the person—not infuriate him!

It's not so much what you say, as the way you say it. And please bear in mind that with these suggestions I'm only giving you ideas on how to handle criticism so that it will be resented to a minimal degree. The actual words you use must be yours, not mine: the way in which you utter them should be your manner, not one dictated by me. It's no use acting a part, or 'reading lines'—you must feel its rightness, you must be convinced in yourself, and then you can put it over in your own way, the way that is *you* and will therefore be convincing to the other person too. But simply as examples of the kind of thing I'm driving at—

DON'T tell a man he's acted like a prize idiot. Explain how he could have handled the affair to better advantage.

DON'T say to your wife: 'You look terrible in that dress!' Try something more like: 'It's lovely. But I wish you'd wear the green one tonight. That shade of green's *terrific* on you . . .'

IF you have no alternative but to issue a really stern criticism, think of a way to sweeten the pill with a simultaneous pat on the back. For instance: 'Joe, that was a fine job you did on Tuesday. But look—this business yesterday . . .'

Above all never forget the golden rule: *if it isn't likely to help—don't voice it!*

The basis of all these do's and don'ts is to be found in the pages which you have already read. Because remember that underlying all purposeful attitudes to other people is:

(*a*) being interested in them,
(*b*) understanding them.

From knowledge of yourself springs understanding of others, and from understanding grows tolerance. When it's your job to analyse another person's behaviour and decide whether criticism can be both purposeful and justified, an understanding of what motivated that person's conduct is a first essential.

To *understand and tolerate* is not the same thing as to *accept*. But with tolerance and understanding you are able to criticize—when you have to—in a just and constructive manner.

And there's a long-term bonus in this, too . . . *The more constructive your criticism, the less you will need to criticize at all!*

(1) Are you easily irritated?
(2) Are you sensitive to criticism?
(3) Do you dislike being in the wrong?
(4) If you're in the wrong, are you over-anxious to defend yourself?
(5) When you've offended someone, do you find it difficult to apologize?
(6) Are you more anxious to win an argument than to learn from it?
(7) If someone is rude to you, do you react by being rude in return?
(8) If you meet someone whose views differ from your own, do you feel the need to prove that yours are right?
(9) Are you prepared to accept the views of someone whom you dislike if he produces a convincing argument?
(10) In considering what's right and what's wrong, are you certain that your personal judgement of moral standards is reliable?

CHAPTER EIGHT

AT THE RECEIVING END . . .

We've been talking about criticism from the point of view of the man who hands it out. What about the other angle—the man who takes it?

Let's admit that nobody *enjoys* being criticized. Our natural reaction is to resent it, to throw up a defence of self-justification or reciprocal aggression. Even when we know it's deserved, we'd rather do without it.

Why? Largely because you have a certain image of yourself, and being put on the carpet tends to tarnish that image.

If you glance back at the maturity test (page 12) you'll find questions 6 and 12 respectively are:

(6) Do you make up flattering stories about your-self?

(12) Do you think you're better than others believe you to be?

Affirmative answers to these questions, or even 'yes-and-no' answers, suggests a degree of immaturity. And it's pretty obvious that the man whose honesty compels him to answer 'yes' to both questions will hardly revel in having his faults spelt out to him. Referring back again—page 14—I've emphasized that nobody is 100 per cent mature. So the chances are that *you* will resent criticism more than you'll welcome it.

And that's an understatement. If as a psychiatrist I found myself talking to someone who positively enjoyed being criticized, I'd look for other signs of masochism, and be puzzled if I didn't find some!

However—as we've already concluded, criticism can be justified and helpful. Since you're not perfect, but fallible and capable of error, you must occasionally be prepared to face the music.

It may not be justified—but nine times out of ten there is no smoke without fire. The criticism may be offered in a clumsy and aggressive manner. But if it has genuine justification allowances can be made for poor presentation and you'll be able to accept its *constructive* value.

Even if it is put badly and it infuriates you, you can think about it more clearly in retrospect when you have cooled down a bit. And if there's something to be learnt, for goodness' sake—learn it! Perhaps there was a brawl —threats—a slammed door . . . such things do happen, even to those who should know better. Of course the immediate result is negative and unhelpful. But when you realize you were in the wrong, then there'll be gains to set against the losses. You don't *have* to go back and say, 'I'm sorry, I won't do it again'; merely making that resolution in your own mind will help to avert a repetition of similar behaviour.

But why *not* apologize—if you know the fault was yours? If you know it, you can bet your life others involved know it too. So what are you losing?

In fact you can do better: admit responsibility, take the sting out of impending criticism before it is even voiced. To do so is certainly not weakness—it is strength, and it will be seen as such.

Let me make one thing clear. The points I'm trying to make aren't directed only at employers and employees. They apply to any situation, environment or relationship. In the home, for instance, in rows between husband and wife, altercations between parents and children—the principles and the do's and don'ts are equally applicable. They apply to all of us.

Admitting your defects

The fact that you decided to get this book, and are reading it, is fair indication you still have things to learn. You are admitting to yourself there is room for self-improvement. Why be ashamed to admit it to others?

To be willing to listen, to recognize you don't know everything—and that you never *will* know everything —is an indication of maturity. The other extreme is the spoilt child who sulks whenever he's taken to task. There are people, unfortunately, who go through their lives in that condition.

Most of us are capable of reverting to this childlike behaviour under certain circumstances, especially when caught off-balance. You're a bit off-colour; the morning post brought a chill reminder of an unpaid bill; it's pouring with rain and your barber has pointed out that the bald patch on the back of your head isn't getting any smaller. Your boss sends for you, and before you've even shut the door he starts testily, 'Now look here, Smith——'

Boom! You've hit the roof!

When that policeman stopped me, if he hadn't spoken first and in the tone I've described, I would have blustered, sworn that I *did* give the right signal and that the other fellow was driving too fast, etc. The policeman would have known I was lying, I'd have known he knew it, and I'd have looked twice as stupid as I did to start with. It would also have annoyed him, and that wouldn't have helped. But from the way he reacted, it's plain what my attitude should have been even if he'd been no more than an angry copper 'going by the book'. I was to blame: we both knew it. I should have said, 'Officer, I just did a crazy thing. I don't know why, I don't usually act like a dangerous lunatic, and all I can say is, I'm sorry.'

As he so rightly pointed out, *we all make fools of ourselves sometimes*.

We have to recognize—even though we may not know enough about psychology to understand unconscious motivations—that our thoughts and behaviour are not determined by our conscious minds alone. This is the reason for our otherwise 'unexplainable' emotional responses to certain subjects. We behave 'out of character'; we say 'I don't know what came over me!'

You must keep this in mind whether you are handing out advice or receiving it. Before offering it, ask yourself whether you are being objective and logical, or over-emotional. Before resenting criticism when it's thrown at you, try to understand why the person giving it feels as strongly as he does. Admittedly, this is not always easy—but it's worth trying!

He may not be acting logically by your standards. But if you can understand why he's so worked up about it, you may be able to de-fuse the situation before it gets out of hand.

So here we are back at the same subject—knowing ourselves, and understanding others. Accepting the simple fact that no two people are alike or think alike: that differences between them do not make one superior to the other. Applying these principles as to how to behave under criticism, we might lay down a few more laws:

(i) Listen. Try to understand.

(ii) Let your critic see you're interested in what he has to say.

(iii) Explain your own angle—if it's likely to help —but *in relation to his*, acknowledging his right to his view-point, arguing *with* him and not *against* him.

(iv) If you're wrong—admit it!

(v) If you're in the right and can prove it, don't be too 'holy' about it. Remember (1) you can win a battle and lose the war; (2) that the stronger your position, the more magnanimous you can afford to be.

(vi) If he's right, give him the credit for having shown you where you were going off the rails. A word of thanks costs far less than the dividends it can produce.

In a nutshell . . . *Why make an enemy when you could use the opportunity to make a friend or cement a friendship?*

ARE YOU IN TOUCH WITH THE WORLD AROUND YOU? (5-minute quiz)

(1) Give yourself 60 seconds to name 3 major items of international news which you have read about during the last fortnight. (3)

(2) Give yourself 30 seconds to write down the names of 5 members of your country's present government (5)

(3) Give yourself 30 seconds to name the 6 world leaders who in your opinion share most responsibility for the maintenance of peace. (6)

(4) Take 60 seconds now to write down 3 foreign currency equivalents to your own country's monetary unit (3)

(5) Name—in 60 seconds—4 novels published in the last 6 months. (4)

(6) Now take another 60 seconds to put authors' names against the titles. (4) [Maximum score: 25]

If you score 25—which would mean 25 acceptable answers recorded inside the time limit—you're likely to be either a politician or a journalist.

If you score 20 or more, you're reasonably well in touch with what's in progress in the world.

If you score less than 20, you ought to be more closely in touch than you are. Read your daily paper more thoroughly. Make an effort to remember what you've read. If necessary, change to a paper which carries more hard news. Switch over to the current-affairs programme on your radio or TV set.

CHAPTER NINE

SOFTLY, SOFTLY—
catchee monkey . . .

From the sometimes negative area of criticism, I want to turn to the positive one of *persuasion*. You will find it is a subject which covers an enormously wide field of human activity. For instance—you've set up your personal target, your goal, but you're unlikely to get to it on your own. Look back to those words of de la Rochefoucauld's (page 49). Wherever you're going, you'll need the help and co-operation of other people. The more help you get, the faster you'll travel. Some of it will come to you voluntarily—if you're lucky—but most of it you'll have to look for *and attract*.

How? Well, here we go again. *People don't just help people, they help each other . . .*

A salesman who wants to be successful won't get far by trying to force goods on a housewife merely because he wants her money. He's got to persuade her that she needs what he's offering. A politician won't win votes by saying: 'This is what I think is good for you, so that's what I'll see you get.' If he wants them to vote for him he must say: 'I know this is what you want, and I would like you to put me in a position where I can get it for you.'

A girl who wants a man to marry her is unlikely to get her way by telling him it's time he popped the question. But she will if she makes herself so necessary to him that he'll *want* to marry her.

There is a saying, 'You can lead a horse to water, but you can't make it drink' ... *Rubbish! All you have to do is make sure the animal is thirsty.*

We are indeed back on familiar ground, because this again is a matter of understanding people. To persuade a person to do what you want him to do, you must understand his needs well enough to put the proposition in a way that appeals to him. To get his help, first discover how he needs *yours*.

Creating the right climate

You want people to react pleasantly and helpfully, don't you? Of course you do. So why not create a climate in which they'll want to do so? If you want a girl to like you, let her know you like *her*. If you want a man's interest in what you're doing, show interest in what *he's* up to ...

Trickery?

Nonsense. Does a farmer sow a field with dandelions if he wants a crop of wheat?

There's nothing dishonest in setting out to build an atmosphere in which relationships flourish and positive results can be achieved. To behave otherwise is plain stupidity! There's nothing selfish about it. First, because the benefits are reciprocal, and not one-sided. Second, because what may start as an attempt to show interest in another human being often develops into a real and lasting interest.

I wonder if you've ever had an experience of *this* kind ...

You're at a cocktail party. There's a man across the room whose name you didn't catch when you were introduced. You don't much like the look of him, and feel little desire to make closer acquaintance. It would be easy to do so, of course—all you have to do is walk across the room. But there are plenty of people whom you already know, to whom you can chat without any kind of effort—so what the hell!

Later, when the party has thinned out and changed shape, you find yourself close to the stranger. Perhaps the drinks have reduced your social inhibitions. You move over to him and introduce yourself, and this time you get each others' names right. Within a few moments you're sharing a conversation with someone whom you're glad to have met. To your surprise he interests you, and he seems interested in you. Believe it or not, you *like* each other.

What has this to do with the art of persuasion? Nothing, really. It's only an indication of the fact that the ground for worthwhile human relationships is nearly always fertile. All you have to do is *use it*.

You will never be in a position to persuade anyone into anything *unless you do*!

Again, you can't effectively negotiate with a man whose point of view you don't understand.

A salesman making his first approach to a new buyer understands this. He holds his fire until he thinks he knows what makes his customer tick, then uses that knowledge to decide on his selling tactics.

In salesmanship, of course, there *are* tricks. Gambits such as, 'Of course, *this* model is a bit beyond your price range . . .'—banking on the customer resenting the suggestion that he can't afford the more expensive item and buying it just to prove what a big shot he is. Similarly, I know someone who was an overseas salesman for a firm of London publishers. Some of his books were too highbrow or too technical to sell a single copy even in the best and biggest of bookshops. Except, he discovered, in a very small and scruffy shop which specialized in the more lurid paperback fiction. My friend found the knack by accident: one day, going through his lists with the shopkeeper, he murmured, 'Better skim over these. Not what *your* customers would buy . . .' Can you guess what happened? From that day on he knew he could sell at least one copy of every really 'difficult' book on his list!

But there are plenty of books on salesmanship, books written for salesmen by salesmen. And as I've said before, I'm not addressing any one section of the population. So let's leave sales techniques to sales technicians. The field of 'selling' which concerns us here is—

Selling oneself to others

—which brings us back to the all-important question of *how to deal with people* . . . Knowing yourself, understanding others, making the most of existing relationships and taking every opportunity to establish new ones.

To persuade people into anything at all, you must communicate with them. The most direct means of doing so is speech. And to speak effectively, *persuasively*, whether your audience consists of one person or many, I would like you to consider ten basic rules.

1. *Know what you're talking about, and believe in what you're saying.*

Personal conviction does 'come across'. I discovered this for myself nearly thirty years ago, and remember the occasion particularly well—I was in the dock at the Old Bailey, charged as a criminal under the Common Law.

69

I had written a book called *Love Without Fear*. It has sold approximately four million copies and is still selling. But when first published the Director of Public Prosecutions decided it was an obscene work and instituted proceedings for which I and the publishers should be prosecuted. So I found myself in the dock: and at this time, no one had ever been acquitted at the Old Bailey on such a charge.

Not a cheerful prospect, was it? Not from where I stood, anyway. It might have been an entertaining spectacle for the public, but if you want to know how it feels to be hauled up those steps into the dock under police guard—I can only leave it to your imagination.

I was anxious to go into the witness box and submit myself to cross-examination. I wanted to because I *knew* the book I wrote was not obscene. I believed it had purpose, value, and that there were thousands who needed practical guidance on sexual expression. I was sure that if I could genuinely express my feelings and my own certainty that the charge was unfounded, I would have a chance of convincing the jury and making them think likewise.

My Counsel, a distinguished and experienced K.C., was utterly opposed to my doing anything of the sort. The prosecutor would make mincemeat of me; we'd certainly lose the case, he said.

I felt we'd lose if I didn't. And if we lost, it was I who'd suffer—perhaps receive a prison sentence.

I went into the box and told the truth as I saw it, and I became the first man ever to be acquitted at the Old Bailey on such a charge.

It worked because I was certain of my innocence, and because that certainty 'came across' to judge and jury.

I won't pretend it's one of my fondest memories. In fact it was one of the most unpleasant experiences of my life. But there's a lesson in this story: when you *know* you're right, stick to your guns!

2. *Put what you have to say in relation to your audience's needs and interests*

If that isn't possible or you can't see how to do it, you're wasting your time and breath. On the whole, people would rather talk than listen. If you can't convince them that what you have to say affects them personally, they *won't* listen.

At a time when the world was ringing to some of his greatest and most effective speeches, Sir Winston Churchill remarked to his doctor, 'I don't know about oratory. But I do know what is in people's minds and how to speak to them.'

3. *Never talk in a way others can't follow*

Asking people to listen to you is asking a lot. Expecting them to work hard to understand you is asking a great deal too much. Remember it's not what you say but the way you say it that can be so important. Modesty, together with an air of self-assurance, seldom fails to get a good response.

4. *Never 'talk down' to people*

Everyone wants to be given credit for a modicum of intelligence, to be treated as an adult. A few months ago I walked out of a luncheon club because the guest speaker, a well-known politician, addressed us as if we shared his mental age—roughly ten. I couldn't stand it!

5. *Don't attempt to force ideas on people 'from outside'*

Let the discussion be two-way, so that by the time you reach a conclusion it's not just *your* idea, but theirs as well. If you handle it well enough you may even end up allowing *them* to convince *you*!

6. *Remember other people like to get a word in too*

Why should they listen to your voice if you won't listen to theirs?

7. *But don't just allow them to speak and then go right back to where you paused for breath*

Make them feel what they say matters. Take it into account: amend or amplify your own thesis to include it.

8. *Don't argue against them—argue with them!*

Remember that forceful opposition provokes resistance. The power of leadership lies in *leading*—not in *driving*.

9. *Be flexible in your tactics*

People differ, they don't all react in the same way to the same stimulus. If you see that your usual approach is missing the target, change it—fast!

10. *Beware of flattery*

At least, use it lightly. If you're too 'obvious', the man you're talking to will think you take him for a fool. But when praise is justified, don't be shy of it, put it on thick. If criticism is something necessary, so too is praise. Everyone likes to have his good points maximized, and his faults minimized!

Tricks, you say?

Maybe—but they are ways of communicating with your fellow humans so as to produce the best results for them and for you. What's wrong with that? Don't you want results? Don't I? Doesn't everyone?

But don't just 'go through the motions'—*mean them*! None of the rules I've set down is arbitrary: each is soundly based in the precepts discussed in previous chapters. And the difference between (*a*) treating people as they would like to be treated, and (*b*) trying to pull the wool over their eyes, is—

honesty of purpose

From a warm friendly relationship, dramatic results can be achieved. From a poor one—nothing.

CHAPTER TEN

WHO DO YOU THINK YOU'RE FOOLING?

You might think some of the suggestions I've made are tantamount to telling you to behave dishonestly—to *adopt a pose*.

On the face of it, there's good reason to raise this question. If you feel a natural antipathy towards someone, yet advance an outstretched hand and face wreathed in smiles, you *are* putting on an act, aren't you?

Whereas I've told you that you must *know yourself* and *be yourself*.

How can we reconcile these contradictory proposals? Well, I'd like to start by showing you another piece of film—actually two pieces. As before: the same action, with significant variations in dialogue . . .

The scene is a cocktail party. About twenty people in groups of various sizes, all with glasses in their hands and most of them talking. But one man looks a bit out of the swim. His name is White. He's on his own, hovering diffidently on the party's fringe. The clock's hands stand at 6.45.

Now it's 7.30, and quite a few people have gone home. The man who seemed so alone before is now deep in conversation with one of the remaining guests.

WHITE: Heavens, look at the time! I must be off——

74

BLACK: Oh, you don't have to go yet, do you? Hang on a few more minutes. I'd like to hear more about——
WHITE: No, I have to go. Sorry, but——(*He smiles.*) I've enjoyed this talk, too. Perhaps some other time?
BLACK: I'd like that. Are you in the phone book? (WHITE *nods.*) I'll be in touch, then. Perhaps we could persuade you to come over for a meal . . .

(*We see* WHITE *saying good-bye to his host and hostess, then departing.* BLACK *glances round, and his wife comes up to him.*)

MRS. BLACK: Your good deed for the day, darling?
BLACK: What d'you mean?
MRS. BLACK: How you managed to stick that frightful bore for nearly half an hour——
BLACK: Actually, he's nothing of the sort. He's damned interesting to talk to. You'll be surprised. As it happens, I've sort of half invited him to . . .

We'll cut at this point. Now to see the other version we needn't go right back to the beginning, only to the point where White has left the party and Black is joined by his wife.

MRS. BLACK: Your good deed for the day, darling? (BLACK *only chuckles.*) How you managed to stick that frightful bore for nearly half an hour——
BLACK: His name's White. *George* White.
MRS. BLACK: Well, bully for him!
BLACK: He's on the Council.
MRS. BLACK: So what's that to——
BLACK: Chairman of the Planning Committee. If you remember, there's some question of that field behind our house being used for a——
MRS. BLACK: Darling, you're a *genius*!

75

Our camera can fade out, now, on the Blacks' craftily smiling faces.

In the first shot, it's true that Black was putting on an act when he engaged White in conversation. But his object was constructive, to create an atmosphere in which a friendly relationship might develop. Perhaps he was only taking pity on a lonely person. His 'pose' was a bridging operation aimed at achieving a worthwhile purpose. As such, it was entirely legitimate—basically because the intention behind it was honest.

But in the second case, Black's attitude was less social 'pose' than deliberate 'con'. His object was dishonest, and to secure a selfish advantage he will have to continue in a dishonest relationship. Between this and the first example is all the difference in the world.

We all strike attitudes, at times. We have to.

When you're leaving a function like that one in the film sequence, don't you invariably tell your host and hostess that it was a lovely party?

Of course you do. But if you were entirely honest, there'd be some occasions when you'd have to say 'Goodnight. Such a *dreary* evening . . .'

Life would be impossible if we always spoke the truth, the whole truth and nothing but the truth. A 'white lie' is often no more than kindness. When a pose originates in an honest intention, it seems to me that the pose is honest too.

We're all actors

—and, as we quoted Shakespeare before, 'each man in his time plays many parts'.

Every time a man puts on a dark suit and a bowler hat and hooks an umbrella over his arm, he's adopting a role, a pose.

The only time you were entirely 'natural' in your behaviour was when you were lying in your pram. Once beyond that stage, you began to learn the patter necessary for the various roles in life. For instance . . .

Professional pose. A man whose business acumen and energy have pushed him into the top echelons of commercial life may find it necessary to adopt a 'tycoon pose'. He'll dress the part, adopt appropriate mannerisms, and he may hire a chauffeur although in fact he prefers to drive himself. All this is the camouflage he may need in order to do a job where colleagues and subordinates react more satisfactorily to one who 'looks the part'.

Religious–social pose. You have to attend the funeral of someone whom you never knew all that well. You barely knew he was alive, so why should you be expected to show grief at his death? Still, you wear your darkest clothes, and you manage to look as solemn as if it was your best friend in that box.

Do I hear an indignant protest—'It's only a matter of showing respect'?

So it is—respect to the conventions of society. Not to the man in the box: from where he is, he couldn't care less if you turned up in red pyjamas. But all right, it *is* a matter of 'showing respect'. And to do so, you *adopt a pose*—in dress, and in manner.

With so many poses forced on you, there isn't all that much time left in which you can openly be yourself, the plain unvarnished *you*. So for heaven's sake don't waste that time by making up poses of your own!

To yourself, you must *be yourself* all the time. If you catch yourself out in an unnecessary pretence, reflect on it and try to discover why you did it, what your motivation might have been. Irrational behaviour doesn't stand on its own—it's a symptom of something wrong behind it. In terms of understanding yourself you must get to grips with whatever this cause is—before it gets too firm a grip on *you*!

Remember that however much of a disguise you may find it necessary to adopt in one role or another, if you ever begin to fool *yourself* you're heading for trouble.

Suppose you are that big-business man, for instance. When you get home and shed your Savile Row apparel, you can shed the 'part' with it. You become what in fact you've been all the time, under the disguise: yourself—husband—father—human being. The person whom your family and closest friends know as *you*. If it isn't easy and natural for you to revert in this way—if it isn't a positive pleasure to do so—you're losing control. It's time you came to terms again with the person you really are. Take a long holiday—and a long, close look at yourself and where you're heading. Do it now, before you can't even recognize that face in the bathroom mirror!

Anything that doesn't fit perfectly, causes irritation. Similarly, since all poses are unreal, any attempt to wear one permanently must damage the individual.

One other point.

We've discussed the 'honest' pose—the bridging operation intended to transform a negative relationship into a positive one. This, we've seen, is not only legitimate but socially necessary.

But is honesty of purpose the only criterion?

I think you must have a degree of realism too.

There's no point in attempting the impossible. If there is no chance of you and George White 'getting on', you will achieve nothing by trying to force yourself into a friendly relationship. The absence of common ground or the antipathy may be of your making, or his, or due to circumstances neither of you can alter. If that's the situation, don't fight it.

There's every reason not to. If there's no hope of making a friend, you are wasting your time.

I know I've said you should take every opportunity to make a friend. I stand by that precept. But in a case where there *is no* opportunity—and where you're sure there's no hope of success, what the hell!

Like that target you've set yourself. There's never the slightest point in aiming for what you know you can't achieve. *The successful man picks targets he can hit —and people with whom he can work!*

Gossip

Every human being lives in communication with other humans. And not in a series of watertight compartments, with each relationship kept separate. We introduce our friends to each other, and they talk about each other. Thus we build cross-channels of communication which relate thousands of relationships to thousands of others; it's a kind of cross-pollination which eventually links all the myriads of individuals and individual relationships into the constantly shifting mass of human society.

We communicate, therefore, not only *with* people, but also *about* them. We *gossip.*

It's a sign of our interest in others, it's an outlet for that interest, and it's entirely healthy. Secrecy—separation from society, lack of interest in it—is *un*healthy.

But there are temptations and dangers involved in the gossip business, and for your own sake as well as others there are certain rules you should stick to. Here they are . . .

(1) The information you pass on should be reasonably truthful. I say 'reasonably' because you can be allowed a little poetic licence—licence to put the information over in an entertaining way!

(2) If the information concerns something of which you disapprove, it's less information, and more behind-the-back criticism. It's almost certainly none of your business. If it *is*, talk to the person immediately concerned —not someone who isn't!

(3) If it's untrue, then it isn't gossip, it's malice— possibly legal slander, and in any case a social evil.

(4) If you've been told it by someone else and you think it might be untrue, let it stop with *you*. If you pass it on, you're morally (and legally) as responsible for the lie as if you'd started it.

(5) If in doubt, apply the golden test: ask yourself, 'Could I, at a pinch, repeat this back to the person whom it concerns?'

Perhaps it would be slightly embarrassing: you might have to explain the joke, and so on. But if even with a touch of awkwardness you *could* answer the question 'What's that you were saying about me?' then you can't have been doing much harm.

If it's something you *couldn't* repeat back, the best advice I can give you is

shut up!

Or you'll lose those friends which this book is aimed at showing you how to keep. Could *you* regard someone as a friend if you heard he'd been maligning you to other people?

(1) Do you have a clear picture of yourself—strengths, weaknesses, abilities, etc.?

(2) Do you think other people share that view of you?

(3) When you hear other people's views of you or of your behaviour, do you pay as much attention to critical comments as you do to praise?

(4) Do you feel consciously in control of your life—or does it seem to be shaped and altered by events more than by your own will?

(5) Have your career decisions usually proved right?

(6) Are you quick to seize opportunities when they occur?

(7) Do you worry much about things which have already happened?

(8) Are you often anxious about what *might* happen?

(9) Do you think your friends see you as an optimist —or as a pessimist?

(10) If you dislike Smith and hate Jones, do you think this attitude is primarily damaging to them—or to you?

CHAPTER ELEVEN

YOU AND YOUR MARRIAGE

The word could as well be 'cohabitation' as 'marriage', because I'm discussing the relationship between men and women who live together, share each others' lives. Whether they have been married in a church, licensed in a state registry office, or simply decided to share a bed-sitter, is unimportant. It makes no difference—for the purpose of this discussion—how it came about that they are now in a marriage-type relationship. The fact is simply that they *are*: that a close human, emotional and sexual relationship exists between them. And since this book is primarily concerned with human relationships, *all* relationships have their place in the discussion.

In the next chapter I shall be discussing the changing face of the institution of marriage, why it is essential for *you* to be aware of the marital/sexual 'wind of change'. But initially I want to talk about the 'nuts and bolts' of the long-term man/woman relationship—which, at the present time, is as likely as not to be of the conventional variety.

These 'poses' which we've been discussing: the last state on earth in which you can get away with a disguise of any sort is in marriage. When you share the same bed and perhaps the same bath-water, you *can* only be yourselves.

No poses, pomposities or pretences—each partner sees the other exactly as he/she is. Isn't such total 'naturalness' one of the joys of the relationship? But naturally it's a lot easier if both like what they see!

The only way to ensure it is to make a realistic choice of partner. To be sure you truly *know* the person you are going to marry, and that he/she has an honest appreciation of *you*. To be certain you are choosing someone who is neither invested with qualities which you're imagining—and that can easily happen when you're 'in love', seeing everything through rose-tinted spectacles—nor putting on a front calculated to attract. (Of course, each partner is out to attract the other: I'm talking about *deception*.)

If you try to put over an act with the person you hope to marry, by pretending to be something other than you are, you're only fooling yourself. The deception won't last much beyond the honeymoon: you'll be found out, and found wanting. Much better play it straight—*be yourself*, and trust in that 'self' having sufficient attraction to win the day. *If it hasn't, you'll be well out of it, because the marriage would have started on an insecure foundation.*

Horses for courses . . .

The question of choosing the right partner comes down again to *knowing yourself* in order that you should be capable of selecting the kind of person with whom you'll have a reasonable chance of making the marriage work. However good-looking, intelligent, capable, reliable, etc., a person is, that is not necessarily an indication that he/she will be *right for you*. Look, for instance, at this example: the wedding of masochist to masochist would create obvious difficulties right from the first day of the honeymoon. Similarly, one sadist would find little but frustration in marrying another sadist. On the other hand, the marriage of a sadist to a masochist *could* be a roaring success.

If the roars didn't wake the neighbours.

Not every man wants a 'perfect' wife. Quite recently someone said to me, 'My wife's an angel'. I was about to congratulate him, when he added crossly, 'Who the hell wants to be married to an angel?'

Many would ask nothing better. But the man who asked me that question would have preferred a girl who would present him with challenge and excitement, rather than cater only to his domestic needs. He'd put up with a wife who might flirt with other men, a girl he'd have to keep his eye on (discreetly) when they went out to parties together. The sort of wife who, if she said she was going to spend the weekend with her mother, *might* be going in quite a different direction—as *he* might too, if he told her he was going fishing.

If you're the kind of man who wants to know that at whatever time he gets home the 'little woman' will be waiting with his socks darned and the house all neat and tidy, you may find it difficult to understand the husband I've just mentioned. He, on the other hand, might groan at the thought of being tied to *your* girl.

On the subject of angels—has it ever occurred to you that angels and devils are only half-persons?

As we all have good and bad in us, both influences should be allowed to emerge—to be experienced—if we are to live our lives to the full. Similarly, we shouldn't be surprised to find both 'sweet and sour' in other people. Perfection is with the dodo or the unicorn—and knowing that there is no such animal, we should persuade ourselves to accept, in any meaningful relationship, that the other person is as he or she is. *It is completely pointless, and often destructive, to see our partner in comparison with what we would like him/her to be.*

So we're back again to the truth—simple as it may be—that *people differ* . . .

The 'obvious' choice isn't always the right choice. To make one that will work, you must know what you *are*, what you need, the sort of person you can live with and who can live with you. And before you decide on a liaison as permanent (in intention, anyway) as marriage, you must be sure that each understands what sort of life you intend to make together. (This is a subject to which I shall be returning in the next chapter.)

Marriage is a gamble, and love is the least important factor in the decision. That is to say, if you want to marry in love you must take care to love the right person—the right person for *you*. Since 'love' is a completely involuntary emotional condition, it's plain what an enormous part is played by sheer chance in the success or failure of marriages based on it. If you don't set out to select your partner in as realistic and as cautious a manner as possible, you might as well make the choice in a Paul Jones or pick a name out of a hat.

I've come across plenty of couples who might have been happier if they'd chosen their partners that way instead of the way they did.

To the marriage relationship, every precept we've already discussed applies . . .

Know yourself—and *be* yourself.

Know your partner—understand him/her—allow him or her to be what they are and not what you would like them to be.

Don't think that how *you* feel about something matters more than how your partner feels.

85

Don't try to win all the arguments. Not even if you *can*!
Criticize only when you have to—and then with care.
Remember persuasion is better than coercion. It's more acceptable—and more likely to work!

In the closest of all human relationships, these principles are more vital than anywhere else. 'Charity begins at home'—so does every waking day. Never think, 'We know each other too well for that kind of thing to matter'. No relationship is ever so close that it can't be improved—or so 'safe' that it doesn't need constant thought to *keep* it safe.

Even without going so far as improving the relationship, simply to maintain it in the face of change and time's passage calls for effort, a sense of deliberate purpose. It's a true saying in most circumstances that 'familiarity breeds contempt'. In marriage, familiarity is therefore an occupational hazard! A Trojan horse, right in the centre of the institution!

Oh, there's plenty to guard against . . .

If you don't make the effort, why should your partner? Nobody gets more out of a relationship—in the long run—than they put into it.

The sexual relationship

A physical partnership is just another human relationship, and the fact that it's sexually based doesn't change the rules. Sex is no great mystery imposing new elements of hazard—if to you there *is* any mystery, I suggest you ask a good bookseller to supply you with one of several books I've written on the subject. You'll find them listed in the front of this one.

We've been talking a lot about human relationships. Now we're still discussing the same subject—only in this specific area the bond between the partners happens to be sex. So let's take the same rules and precepts which we've established for human relationships in the general sense, and feed them—together with patterns of sexual motivation and behaviour—into our imaginary computer. Press the 'answer' button, and we'll see what it gives us.

(1) The first essential is *consideration*. To understand and respect your partner's needs, likes, dislikes.

(2) To understand not only the physical pleasures, aversions, etc., but the emotions and emotional needs which motivate and accompany them.

(3) Consciously and deliberately to use such understanding to maintain and improve your relationship isn't trickery. Sex itself is a trick—nature's way of tricking you into (*a*) having children, (*b*) building the family relationship in which your children can safely be reared. The more tricks you know and use, the more likely you are to succeed!

(4) To please, and satisfy physical and emotional needs, to be so motivated as *to want to do so*, you must have an attitude which is (*a*) unselfish, (*b*) reasonably intelligent. Women's understanding being more intuitive than men's, means that men will have to give more conscious thought to the sexual relationship, in order to reach the same conclusions!

(5) Sexual love is not just a matter of performance. Of course technique can be improved—and where there's room for improvement, it *should* be. (If you're a golfer, don't you try to improve your game?) But what matters far more than technique is warmth, emotion, feeling—in one shorter word, *love*. And remember it's how the end-result reaches your partner that counts. So for heaven's sake— or rather for your own

and your partner's—realize that in love there is no place for shyness, reticence, the disguising or suppression of emotion.

(6) Brains as well as genitals are involved in the sexual act. A woman even when she's tired or 'out of sorts' can without much effort take part in sex by 'making herself physically available'. A man in similiar circumstances has to have an operative penis before he can act.

(7) Similarly, it's a serious although common mistake to measure 'love' by physical reaction. Because your partner seems less sexy than you'd like him/her to be—he doesn't get an erection as quickly or as frequently, or she isn't as responsive as she used to be —doesn't mean that you are loved any the less.

It *may* even mean the love is greater! But probably 'love' has nothing to do with it. Both men and women get tired, or depressed. Worries are sometimes difficult to shed when you're tired at the end of the day. And couples get used to each other, so that the degree of visual and tactile stimulation is smaller, more easily superseded by other preoccupations in the mind. This has nothing to do with affection or lack of affection. Nor is it anything to be ashamed of. Least of all is it anything for which to blame your partner!

If all you're thinking about is speed and intensity of physical response, you could get that, probably, from a total stranger. There'd be nothing of 'love' involved. So 'love' hasn't necessarily anything to do with this, has it?

(8) Don't be discouraged because from time to time your relationship runs into heavy weather. *It's bound to.* First, because all human behaviour—including sexual—runs in cycles. If feelings are particularly warm at this moment, they'll probably be cooler next week.

And vice versa. Second, because—here it comes again!
—*people differ*. No two intelligent people can live together without finding areas of disagreement. Even if
the differences are intense, fundamental, why should
they disturb the relationship as a whole? Do you
imagine you have an obligation to ape your partner's
thoughts, beliefs, habits, tastes?

If you say, 'We never quarrel', I take it as evidence
that your relationship is shallow, you don't know each
other well enough to have discovered the areas of
mutual antipathy. Or, you are so insecure in your relationship that you must *avoid* those areas.

(9) Finally, here's a truth worth remembering:

Only idiots are happy all the time!

Be your age!

Marriage, like every other human relationship, is
two-way. If you find things dull, do you imagine *she's*
finding them exciting?

You've been taking each other for granted—like
pieces of furniture. You've nothing much to say to each
other. Love-making has become so uninteresting that
you'd as soon do without it.

You know darned well—if you can look at the situation honestly, objectively—that this isn't all her/his
fault. So instead of either baling out or resignedly accepting the continuance of monotony, why not do something positive to retrieve the situation?

Just as you've been learning to assess your personality, now take stock of your marriage. Sit down and
work out what's good about it and what's not so good.
What would you like to change? What would you prefer
not to lose?

Try answering these questions:

(1) Would I like to be unmarried?

(2) If I was unmarried now, would I marry again?

(3) If I did, what sort of partner would I look for this time?

(4) If I found such a person and married her, could I be sure that in five or ten years' time I'd be more content than I am now?

(5) Is that chance worth taking, in relation to what I'd be doing to my family?

When you are answering these questions, keep 'wishful-thinking' out of your mind. Face facts clearly, honestly. And now answer these:

(6) Given the opportunity, would I be unfaithful to my wife?

(7) Would I accept her being unfaithful to me?

(8) If the answer to six is 'yes', and the answer to seven is 'no', how can I explain such an attitude—even to myself?

(9) Am I dissatisfied with our sexual relationship?

(10) Is the fault hers, mine, or shared?

(11) Is it possible we could do something to improve the situation?

(12) Would I want to if it *were* possible?

(13) Do I love her?

(14) Do I ever tell her I love her?

(15) If I had the chance to start this marriage again from scratch, would I take it?

There are no marks, no prizes! Your answers to these questions will tell you clearly enough what the situation is. You probably knew it to start with: but sometimes a little clear diagnostic thought is enough to clarify something you didn't know you knew.

Of course, there are marital problems and situations which don't answer to such general formulae. Marriages break down for specific causes as well as for general ones, and sometimes break-up is the only way out of an intolerable situation. But a high proportion of marriages simply 'get tired', and this is the common ailment which I'm discussing.

What's that? You've 'been a good husband'? What do you mean by that?

Oh, I see. You mean you've been *faithful*?

Well now, listen. There is a greater crime than infidelity. It's called *cruelty*.

To be cruel, it isn't necessary to use physical violence. You don't even have to raise your voice. Towards a woman who loves you, the weapon that draws most blood, causes most pain, is *indifference*.

For instance—when she speaks to you and you look up, glancing in her direction, do you look *at* her as you used to do? Or do you look *through* her?

Can you expect a women to be responsive when there's nothing for her to respond to?

BE YOUR OWN ANALYST: 6

Imagine you've been dead for five or ten years:

Now picture in turn your

    (*a*) wife/husband
    (*b*) children (5–10 years older, remember!)
    (*c*) closest personal friend
    (*d*) closest business acquaintance

Try to visualize them one at a time as they are questioned by your would-be biographer, who asks each —in strict privacy—the following questions:

(1) What sort of person was he/she?
(2) Did you admire him/her?
(3) (Alternatively) Why not?
    (Alternatively) What was it you most admired?
(4) What would you say were his/her major faults?
(5) What did he/she contribute most to *your* life?

This is a tough one, isn't it? It calls for the use of imagination, acceptance of the fact you will one day be dead, and quite a bit of time, concentration and honesty to work out the answers. But you'll find the exercise worthwhile—it may reveal a few more new facts about yourself.

CHAPTER TWELVE

MARRIAGE *À LA MODE*

I wrote in the last chapter, 'you must be sure that each of you understands what sort of life you intend to make together'.

By that I didn't mean you should decide in advance whether to live in town or country, have two cars or one, etc. I was thinking in much more basic terms—of the fundamental structure of the relationship. *Because we are beginning to realize, nowadays, that there is more than one way in which a man and a woman can share a life.*

To start with, consider for a moment what are—or were—the basic principles on which 'conventional' marriage, as an institution, was established.

(1) Men and women needed each other, sexually and emotionally—and for the practical purpose of having a family.

(2) Women weren't going to risk getting pregnant without some guarantee of security—protection —for themselves and their children.

(3) Men weren't prepared to offer that guarantee unless sure of getting full possession of what they were 'buying'. In effect, they were concerned that they shouldn't find themselves supporting children sired by another man.

So each party to the deal required some form of contract, and the answer came up as 'marriage'. Each obtained what they were after, and in return promised to fulfil their share of the bargain.

Of course, there were drawbacks to the system too. Neither man nor woman is designed emotionally or biologically to spend a whole lifetime with just one sexual partner. Signing the marriage contract, therefore, was to accept restrictions—restrictions which were certainly not 'natural'. They could be borne comparatively easily by some, less easily by others. And to those for whom the restrictions (lifelong monogamy, 'fidelity') were a really heavy burden, the following alternatives presented themselves:

1. *Acceptance of the contractual terms—and simultaneous acceptance of possible sexual frustrations.*

The consequences don't necessarily add up to a successful marriage. Far from it! Frustrations produce psychological imbalance, leading to psychiatric disorder. Their inhibiting influence also helps to explain the market for pornography, the popularity of strip clubs, and other commercial exploitation of the prurience which lies behind so many stiff upper lips, under so many well-brushed bowler hats.

The alternative is—

2. *Cheating on the contract.*

The complications here are so vast, varied and complex that it would be impossible to cover them all in the space we can afford. What is basically wrong is that it *is* cheating. There are areas of emotional trauma to the people involved. For instance, the 'other woman' is left high and dry after having served as an outlet for a husband's frustrations, while the relationship between husband and wife suffers at its very roots from the injection of dishonesty.

94

We have already discussed the necessity for honesty in human relationships. How can a relationship stay close, deep or meaningful when one partner is cheating on the very terms on which the relationship is based?

Winds of change

There are circumstances under which detailed rules, laws and regulations have been outgrown and no longer acceptable.

In primitive times, simple truths needed to be illustrated with crude simplicity. For instance, whereas nowadays anyone but an imbecile would understand the phrase 'do as you would be done by', it was necessary 2000 years ago to say 'an eye for an eye, a tooth for a tooth'.

As civilization extends itself and people become more highly civilized, more and more of what was formerly locked in cast-iron 'commandments' is left to an individual's own sense of right and wrong, fair and unfair, workable and unworkable. It isn't a matter of some authority relaxing the rigour of social regulations: people don't wait for that to happen, but instead assume the latitude and responsibility for themselves.

Of course, not all are capable of carrying such a responsibility. None the less, this is the present pattern, the direction of social evolution . . .

Acceptance of personal responsibility

Evolving new attitudes towards personal freedom doesn't necessarily rule out the 'conventional' marriage. If you want that kind of relationship and are prepared to keep the required promises, naturally you have the right to choose such a way of living together.

And millions are likely to continue to opt for that.

But as time goes on—and in this area patterns of thought and behaviour change quickly—more and more people take quite a different view of the shape which their sexual and emotional relationships should assume. Many will be thinking—indeed, *are* thinking—on the following lines:

1. My relationship with another person is *our* business. Neither Church nor State can effectively tell us how we should relate to each other. We can see all around us the wrecks and remnants of 'conventional' marriage. If we stick to our personal standards rather than to the book we can't do worse than that—and we *think* we may do a great deal better.

2. We want to live together, share our lives and futures. We know our relationship will last as long as we both want it to: with luck 'for ever', but we have to be realistic and admit the possibility of failure. If it doesn't work, how can we benefit from its continuance? Whatever relationship we establish is ours—to maintain, or to break. So why deliberately subject ourselves to archaic rules and laws which, if we find it necessary to separate, would oblige one of us to perform an immoral act with possibly a complete stranger in order to qualify for divorce?

Why in fact, should one voluntarily permit the State to destroy one's dignity as a human being?

3. We will survive more happily in a relationship which is free and voluntary than in one hedged with legal or religious regulations. We ourselves are responsible for the existence and continuance of the relationship, and it will mean more to us through being so intrinsic an expression of the way we have chosen to live. We are obliged to buy licences for our television

96

sets, radios, cars and dogs; we reject the right of the State to license our right to love.

This is an outline of the basic thinking behind the decision to cohabit without the formality of marriage. Such a decision would not, of course, suit everyone. But it is being arrived at by more and more people today, and by tomorrow the numbers will have swollen.

There are, of course, important considerations to be worked out. The biggest of these is undoubtedly the care of future children when an 'informal' relationship breaks down. So, for an example of the fact that such problems are capable of solution, let's glance quickly at this one in particular . . .

(*a*) If a legal commitment is considered necessary, parents can contract to support their children.

(*b*) The main *raison d'être* for unmarried parenthood is that the partners believe it has a better chance of lasting than a more formal relationship. On this basis the children would be more secure, not less so, than they would be otherwise.

(*c*) Legalities apart, there is no reason why if the relationship terminates the children should suffer any more than they would if the parents had been married and divorced. Parents love their children: no legal ritual will make any difference to the strength of the love—nor, if it is absent, can any law enforce it! But the law *can* enforce parental responsibility—inside or outside marriage.

The fact is that marriage as we know it is an imposed system which provides certain social safeguards and probably an equal number of hazards and disadvantages. Because we have adhered to this system for so long is no reason to suppose that a different, more free form of marital association, cannot work at least as well.

Permissive marriage

A compromise solution which avoids the extremes of either (*a*) accepting the dangerous frustrations of enforced monogamy, or (*b*) dispensing altogether with conventional marriage ties, is to contract a formal marriage on the mutual understanding that neither partner will expect sexual 'fidelity'.

Such an arrangement involves no dishonesty. Neither fools the other. Each mutually agrees to remain an individual; neither *possesses* the other; and each can have physical relationships with another without damaging the deep personal relationship they share.

Prior agreement to such a form of marriage is of course essential. Every human relationship calls for a 'square deal', and nobody has the right to embark on a 'conventional' marriage relationship and then change it to a 'free association' when the initial closeness has begun to pall. Any such change must come from mutual, not unilateral decision.

Nor is there room for any vestige of the 'double standard'—for the husband to imagine that he can enjoy himself as much as he likes and insist on his wife remaining 'faithful'. As I've said, human relationships are mutual and reciprocal. To express the same thought in a more 'folksy' way, 'what's sauce for the goose is sauce for the gander'.

There are some who can enter honestly and with deep satisfaction into a marriage of this nature. They want to be married to each other, to share each others' lives and raise *their* children. But they also know that they are not by nature monogamous—and they don't see why they should try to be! Modern developments in contraceptive techniques—in particular, of course, the Pill—have made possible these more open patterns of sexual behaviour. Those who want this kind of marriage know that because there is no danger of conception, no element of fraud or 'cheating', *they can have sexual relationships outside their marriage without threatening it in any way*.

And the relationship can be all the healthier for it. If you have neither to suffer frustration nor experience guilt-feelings which arise from 'cheating', you can have a fuller and more complete relationship. And it will be much stronger—*and much more likely to last*.

Youth and the future of marriage

A characteristic attitude of young people today is that honesty in human relationships is of far greater importance and meaning to them than the observance of arbitrary social rules. They believe in *feeling, response, emotion, affection*; and in the honest, frank exchange of emotions.

Later we shall be discussing emotional honesty in greater detail. I'm referring to it here in order to relate it to the changing face of marriage: as a pointer to the likelihood that the rate of change will accelerate during the next few years.

Personally, I happen to believe that such change is for the better. But if you are shocked by the kind of relationship I've been describing, all I ask you to do is to *think* about it, to try to understand; and then to consider this:

(*a*) Because the vast majority of people have stuck to one system for a very long time (blackmailed by the system itself), this is no good reason why, with the development of new social patterns, quite *different* systems should not emerge.

(*b*) *Total honesty in human relationships—if it can be achieved—is worth more than all the Commandments ever uttered!*

To each his own . . .

People differ . . .

One man's meat is another man's poison . . .

Jones wants a conventional marriage, with insistence on mutual 'fidelity'. So Jones must look for a wife among the girls who want that kind of marriage

Smith wants quite a different set-up for *his* marriage relationship. So he'll be looking for a girl whose ideas would fit in with *that* conception of marriage.

This is what it all boils down to. Don't just think of the honeymoon—think of next year, and the year after, and how things will be in ten years' time. Think about what kind of marriage you want. Be sure your prospective partner has the same ideas. Of course time and experience is likely to make you change these ideas —particularly if you were young when you married —but if you discuss them openly and honestly, you will be sure that each knows what the other expects.

I wish you both the best of luck. Believe me, you'll still need it!

CHAPTER THIRTEEN

OBJECT LESSONS

I was talking the other day to Joe, who had just come back from a ski-ing holiday. He was telling me of a couple of incidents which happened to him while he was away. And these were such clear object-lessons for some of the points I've been trying to make in this book, that they are worth relating.

(1) Finding confidence

It was some years since he'd been ski-ing. On the third day he found himself at the top of a steep, icy gully. Looking down its steepness, narrowness and the hard sheen of its ice surface made him catch his breath and wonder whether it wouldn't be safer to take off his skis and walk.

Then he visualized himself making the steep descent. He knew he *could* have managed it years ago; why not now? In his mind's eye he saw where and how he'd turn—every move he'd make. Suddenly imagination merged with reality *and he was sure he could do it.*

And he did. Exactly as the image in his mind had shown him how to.

Lessons

By stopping to think about it, giving his mind time to adjust itself to attaining success, he 'discovered' what the memory-storage section of his brain already knew. His brain worked as a computer, it fed back to him a detailed picture of a performance of which he was capable but which his conscious mind had forgotten. The knowledge was there in the appropriate memory-cells, rather as if it had been recorded on tape. Once the brain-computer played the tape back to him, he knew he could do something which a minute before had seemed impossible and terrifying.

You can use *your* computer mechanism in much the same way. Instead of shying away from some prospect which at first sight seems frightening, face it squarely and calmly. Ask yourself, 'Am I *sure* I can't do it?'

It's possible you can't but it's also more than possible that you can. You'll only find out for certain by trying. You will keep your self-image up to date by consciously and continuously testing yourself and then examining the results.

You won't extend your range by sheltering within the limits you already know. To fulfil yourself, to realize your full potential, you must strive to push those limits further and further back.

(2) Pride and prejudice

The other thing which Joe told me about his ski-ing holiday stems directly from the first.

He'd gone in a party, and they all stayed in the same hotel. Most of them were beginners at ski-ing—certainly none were experts. They were a pleasant lot —convivial, holiday-spirited, easy to get along with.

But on about the fourth day, some who'd been the friendliest of all towards Joe seemed to cool off in their manner towards him. They were less pleased to see him in the hotel bar after ski-ing; less ready to swap anecdotes of the day's adventures on the slopes.

Suddenly Joe realized why.

For the first few days, like the others—he was a beginner. He'd meet them in the course of a descent, wave to them—and probably fall flat on his face as he did so.

Then he began to remember how to ski. That incident on the third day gave him a confidence from which he profited. By now he could pass his acquaintances on the toughest stretches, wave to them and *not* fall down . . .

So in effect he'd ceased to be one of them!

Lessons

There's no logical reason why performance in a sport should influence the degree of a person's social acceptability. But human reactions aren't all that logical, once a situation is affected by a competitive spirit. Isn't it very similar to that business of winning and losing arguments?

In effect—*you cannot demonstrate superiority and at the same time win affection.*

As it happens, Joe was there to ski, and he was much more interested in improving his performance than in building lasting friendships. But he couldn't help being surprised—and at first disturbed—by such a dramatic change in attitude towards him once he began to excel.

The lesson might be: if you want to be liked, don't show off!

Learning from experience

When young you learn by precept, example and instruction: by being told 'This is the right thing to do', 'That is the wrong way to go about it', etc. You have no inbuilt sense of moral values—until you reach the stage of adolescence, at which point the word 'morality' begins to acquire shape and meaning in your questioning, experimenting mind.

You must teach yourself to notice the little 'everyday' incidents which tend to be lost and ignored in the rush of living. From such incidents, from your own and other people's reactions you'll learn much about human behaviour and motivations. Consciously study what goes on around you every day, and you'll be learning about people. *And 'people' includes yourself!*

CHAPTER FOURTEEN

THE ONLY WAY TO HAVE A FRIEND IS TO BE ONE

This well-known saying comes from the writings of Ralph Waldo Emerson, the American nineteenth-century philosopher and poet.

On the face of it, and on the basis that all human relationships are reciprocal, it's a fairly 'obvious' statement. But in practical terms, how can we purposefully set out to *be* a friend and thereby acquire friends?

Well, there are many kinds of friendship: short ones, long ones, deep ones, shallow ones. There are friendships which 'come naturally'—but still need attention if they are to be maintained—and there are those which are deliberately sought and engineered into being. Into this category, of course, come the majority of business relationships.

Different as they are, they are all worthwhile: worth making, maintaining and cultivating.

Why? *Because the more people you know with whom you can purposefully relate your own personality, the more satisfaction you'll get out of living.*

Rules to remember

1. *Never pass up a chance of making a friend*

Regard a new acquaintance as a potential friend, and remember that a friendly approach produces a friendly reaction.

An example of how opportunities can be taken (positive action) or missed (negative action) is in the description (page 74) of the man at a cocktail party and the stranger with whom he strikes up an acquaintance. The two 'get on', and our man leaves the party with a feeling of positive satisfaction in having used an opportunity to make a friend. The friendship may last or it may not. It may produce concrete results—business or social—or none at all. The fact you've acted positively instead of negatively is satisfying either way.

The short cut from 'acquaintanceship' to friendship is:

2. *Show interest in the other person*

One way of demonstrating your interest in people is to remember their names. In England we are bad at this: introductions tend to be mumbled in a perfunctory, hasty manner, whereas in other countries—particularly America and Scandinavia—the custom is to enunciate names loudly and clearly, with the deliberate intent that they should be heard and remembered. When introducing don't just declare the person's name, but say something about him and what he does.

Now this *is* worth working at. It's always impressive to find that someone whom you've met only briefly on a previous occasion knows who you are when next he sees you. When he remembers your name and you don't recall his, you are (a) impressed by his memory, (b) flattered that there was something about you he found worth the effort of remembering, (c) ashamed you weren't able to return the compliment. You may be flattered, but you're at a disadvantage.

Here are some ways in which you can improve your performance:

(a) Listen carefully to an introduction and make a

conscious effort to memorize the name. Not only at the moment of hearing it but afterwards. If you're at a party or a business meeting, for instance, take a glance round the 'new' faces from time to time, and mentally fit names to them.

(*b*) When you're talking to someone to whom you've just been introduced, make a point of using his/her name in the course of conversation. Once you've spoken a name to its owner's face, you're more likely to recall it later.

(*c*) Don't be afraid, if you haven't properly got his name, to ask him to repeat it. If its a difficult one, ask him to spell it. File the name in your memory together with other points which you can associate with the person. Not just physical characteristics—coupling name to face—but whatever you learn about him. The things which interest him, what he does for a living, where he lives, facts about his family, and so on.

In this there are two advantages, First, you will find it easier to remember a 'package' with its label (the name) than remember the label alone. Second, when you meet again you will impress him by knowing not only his name but also—and perhaps more important —his areas of primary interest. I can't think of a better short cut to establishing *his* interest in *you*!

If it is really important to remember a name, why not write it down, together with some reference notes? The physical act of doing this will help you to memorize it.

A lot of trouble? Perhaps so—at first. But if you set out deliberately to expand your capacity for memorizing names and people, you'll acquire the habit of recollection and the effort becomes unnecessary as time goes by.

In any case, taking trouble over people is what this

book is about. To paraphrase slightly what I've said before—why should anyone want to remember *you* if you can't be bothered to remember *him*?

But you'll be doing more than simply memorizing names and faces. In making the effort to achieve that limited objective, you'll find that you are simultaneously taking a positive interest in people as human beings. From narrow intentions, you'll be making significant advances on the whole broad front of human relationships.

3. *If you can't remember a name*

—admit it at once. Apologize for your awful memory, and perhaps even write the name down. Then you'll not be likely to forget it in a hurry. And at the same time you will show that you *want* to know it. Or you could bluff your way through the conversation and hope that something said would bring the name to mind. You might, if you were lucky, have an opportunity of asking someone else.

4. *Let the other person shine*

You will win another man's friendship by letting him feel *his* importance rather than by trying to impress him with *yours*. To do so requires humility, a readiness to allow others to bask in the sun. It costs you little—and it's the surest way to make sure you'll get your turn later!

Methods: (*a*) Let the person talk. Ask him questions about himself. (But not embarrassingly personal questions, of course.)

(*b*) Discover the areas where he is more knowledgeable than yourself. Show interest in those subjects, and give credit for his knowledge of them.

5. *Be tolerant*

Don't be put off by appearances. First impressions are often way off-beam. Ignore gossip and second-hand opinions. Make your *own* assessment of each new acquaintance!

Keep an open mind towards views which may conflict with yours. If you can't accept his opinions, don't assume he's wrong and you're right. The only thing that's certain is that you differ. If necessary, *agree* to differ.

Incidentally, opinions which conflict sharply with one's own are more interesting to discuss than those which coincide with them. If Jenkins and Roberts share identical views, each might as well address *himself*!

Remember that however convinced you are of the rightness of your judgement, you are not entirely the master of your own opinions. All sorts of feelings, emotions, experiences—*unconscious* motivations—influence your ideas and convictions. Your beliefs in what is right, wrong, shameful, delightful, moral, immoral, sinful, etc., are largely the result of early upbringing, a period during which you were (unknowingly) indoctrinated in those beliefs. Such early conditioning means that what you may regard as rational thinking now may in fact be no more than reflex behaviour. Under these powerful, built-in influences it can require great effort to break out into logic and clear reasoning.

The man or woman with whom you are discussing a particular subject may not have been brain-washed in childhood on that subject as you were. Or he/she may have been able to escape from prejudice into relatively unfettered, objective consideration of it.

So *listen*—you could have a lot to learn.

6. *Don't force your own 'rightness' down his throat*

Suppose you're discussing some matter in which you have expertise, specialist knowledge, and the other person is not so well informed. You *know* he's talking nonsense, that he has his facts wrong.

If you confound him flatly and overwhelm him with your superior knowledge—particularly in front of others—you will certainly give him reason to dislike you. (Look back at the section about arguments—how to win gracefully.) You can change his opinion much more effectively by tactful, friendly persuasion than by telling him he's talking out of the back of his neck. Don't declare that what he's said is rubbish —*question whether it may be inaccurate!*

But if there's no way of doing it except by giving him a bit of a jolt, do it in such a manner that he won't lose face, particularly if others are present. If he realizes afterwards that you've taken the trouble to be considerate, he'll not only accept the point you've proved—he'll respect *you*.

When there is a sound, friendly relationship, you can afford to relax some of these rules. A man with whom you are on the same wavelength is unlikely to resent your telling him that he's talking a load of poppycock. To be on such terms is a satisfaction in itself, a big enough satisfaction to make all the earlier application of rules worthwhile.

But there are still a few points worth remembering:

7. *Trust*

Trust breeds trust. Confidence is repaid with confidence. Suspicion, distrust, are wedges between you. To be thought well of by someone, you must think well of him.

And remember—people in whom we show faith are less likely to *break* faith.

8. *Value*

Value the friendship you've established. Let your friends see and know that you appreciate the relationship you share with them. Don't miss opportunities, when they occur, to strengthen the links by asserting or demonstrating that appreciation.

9. *Don't try to 'possess' your friends*

The pattern of friendships in any society, if it were shown diagramatically, would be an enormously intricate web of radiating and crossing lines.

Any man/woman who is a close friend of yours will certainly have friends of his/her own whom you may not like. You may even find it difficult to understand how John, who is your old buddy, can possibly like Michael at sight of whom you break out in a nasty rash.

Who your friends adopt as friends is not your business! Accept the fact that John sees qualities in Michael to which you are blind. It has nothing to do with your friendship with John. Nor should you expect that because John likes you he should also like Charles, another friend of yours.

10. *Actions count most*

One positive action is worth a lifetime of friendly intentions. When you have the opportunity to help a friend, take it without hesitation. Anyone can talk, smile, nod, shake hands, send Christmas cards: but action is *proof* of friendship.

Aristotle said, 300 years before Christ, 'Friends are much better tried in bad fortune than in good'.

11. *Be honest*

In relationships, honesty begets honesty—and the contrary equally applies.

One advantage you derive from a deep, well-founded friendship is that it *permits* you to be honest—to say exactly what you think, to shed pretence and be what you are. Not only for the sake of honesty as a virtue in itself, but because each person in a relationship is a mirror and a sounding-board to the other. From each other's reactions we increase our own self-awareness.

12. *Remain yourself*

Friends become friends for all sorts of reasons: all sorts of people make friends with all *other* sorts. They don't need to share the same views, tastes, likes, dislikes. The strength of a friendship can be measured by the ability of friends to disagree, or to live entirely different kinds of lives—*and remain friends*.

13 *When friends 'fall out'*

When you no longer feel friendly, don't pursue the friendship. Accept the fact that it's over. If you pretend a warmth which is no longer genuine, the relationship becomes dishonest. It's only a short step then from friendship into enmity.

You've still gained something, because no experience is lost to us. Everything that happens to us, good or bad, leaves its imprint even though we ourselves may be quite unconscious of each contribution. So the benefits of a friendship live on after the friendship itself is dead.

14. *A business friendship*

This should be clearly recognized for what it is: a relationship which is made as pleasant and 'human' as possible but which has the primary purpose of serving the commercial interests of each person.

Remember that any attempt to make a more personal relationship out of it can be dangerous. If that should happen 'naturally', well and good, but if you try to force it you may end up with less than you had at the start.

15. Short-term friendships

They have their value, just as do the more permanent variety. If, for example, you and your wife are on holiday and make friends with another couple, this may make the trip more enjoyable. It is an end in itself, an experience in itself too. There's no need to pretend—as people sometimes do in those circumstances—that the relationship is anything but temporary.

An open, natural approach in our relationships stimulates a similar attitude in others. Remember that different kinds of friendship have their particular spans of life, and that a friendship suitable at one period in your life may be totally unsuitable at another. Remember too that friendship can be experienced and enjoyed at all levels—from the most superficial to the most meaningful. The more friends we have, at *whatever* level, the more we fulfil ourselves.

I started this chapter with a quotation from Ralph Waldo Emerson. Let's wind it up with a definition from another American, Elbert Hubbard . . .

> *A friend is a person who knows all about you—*
> *and still likes you*

Could you ask anything better? Could there be anything finer, more valuable to possess?

Think about it. Then ask yourself, how many such friends have I got? How many *might* I have if I deliberately set out to acquire them?

There's only one way to find out. *Start now!*

(1) When you want something badly and decide to go after it, do you stop to ask yourself how those closest to you will be affected?

(2) Do you feel superior, as a person, to your subordiates?

(3) Are you attracted to strong personalities?

(4) Do you enjoy asserting you own personality over a weaker one?

(5) Do you prefer to have decisions made for you?

(6) Do you feel ill-at-ease in the presence of your superiors?

(7) Do you play different 'parts' when you're with different kinds of people?

(8) Do you feel dependent on those closest to you?

(9) Do you feel your friends belong to *you*?

(10) Do you worry about what other people may think of you?

CHAPTER FIFTEEN

BRAIN AND SINEW

Physical and mental health are quite inseparable. I have already made that point, but now let's go further . . .

Complete harmony between mind and body is essential if you want to lead a purposeful, self-fulfilling life.

By knowing yourself, you can establish realistic aims. If you don't shoot for targets within your potential reach, or if you aim for ones beyond your reach, you'll get unhappiness and frustration instead of satisfaction. You will then find it twice as difficult to cope with the pressures of modern life. You will join those who fall easy prey to ulcers, coronaries, depressions, nervous breakdowns. What's the next step? Usually it comes in bright colours and small bottles: pep pills, tranquillizers, and all sorts of drugs.

Pills are no answer. A human being is an indivisible whole—mind plus body. A defect in the mental process can reduce resistance to bodily disease: a disease in the body can upset the balance of the mind.

You know, I'm sure, that mental worry can produce an ulcer in the stomach. That's mind affecting body. To see the process reversed, you know what it's like to wake up with a 'liverish' feeling? You're depressed, short-tempered. That's your liver affecting your mental outlook.

I'm not concerned here with the treatment of disease,

but with the results of failing to live life to the full. The enemy is strictly non-organic: apathy, a vague discontent, disinterest. The sheer weight of monotony, the burden of a seemingly pointless daily round . . .

This has been the malady of the sixties, and it's likely to take an even stronger hold in the next decade.

But you need not succumb to it!

How can you achieve the balanced harmony which is essential if you're going to lead life to the full?

Mental attitudes, as we have seen, affect bodily health, and vice versa. So attention to physical *and* psychological factors is called for. It's not a matter of choosing one or the other—you must use *both*.

Breathing

Air is drawn into your lungs, from which the oxygen is extracted and passed into the bloodstream. The red cells in the blood carry the oxygen to the cells of your body, and they bring back the waste product—carbon monoxide. This process happens with every breath you take.

The rate of breathing is affected by emotional conditions. When your wife's angry with you, notice the speed-up in her respirations. How sudden shock can make you catch your breath. How tension—fear, anger, worry, excitement—makes your heart pound.

Try an experiment. Next time you feel you're about to lose your temper, take long, slow breaths. Keep that going for a minute or so, then see what's happened to that flood of anger.

You can't breathe deeply and remain excited!

A soldier under fire has been known to suffer paralysis of the legs without being physically wounded. How? Because his instinct of self-preservation is screaming at him to run away, while his *conscious* mind fights against that instinctive urge. The battle which takes place inside him is the one that does the damage; the strain is so severe that something has to crack.

I don't need to give any further examples to prove the relationship between mind and body.

The goal is well-being

To keep your body working properly, you must *use* it properly. And there is one thing which, if you can get it right, will correct a host of minor ills, ill-usages ...

Posture

Good posture is all-important to your body's health. If you adopt incorrect posture, you impose strains on certain muscles. When misused long enough, those muscles function inadequately.

You probably realize that when you want to move a limb, your brain signals an instruction to the appropriate muscles to do so: but if that equipment is faulty, the brain's signal won't be properly obeyed. If I may use one more military analogy: when orders from HQ aren't carried out efficiently, what can you expect but chaos?

Stand properly. I don't mean Army-style—chest out, stomach in, eyes bulging with strain. If you stand comfortably but upright, as your body is designed to stand, everything will fit *naturally* into place. For instance, if you stand with your back straight (not stretched or strained, simply upright) and your head up, it isn't easy to stick your stomach out, is it? You don't have to tense yourself to hold it in, because your position is natural and therefore *right*.

If you've been in the habit of standing badly, it may not *feel* right at first. Practise, and it will. Try it in front of a mirror. Your shoulders should be level—not braced back, simply level. The position of your head should be such that you are looking yourself in the eyes. This means that your chin is raised, but not stuck out unnaturally.

When you're standing as you should, it's easy to move suddenly—to turn about, step quickly this way or that. When your position is wrong, the movement will be clumsy and the starting-effort much greater. *It has been worked out that for a person weighing ten stone to start a forward movement it requires an effort of half one foot-pound if his starting posture is correct, and five foot-pounds if it is incorrect.*

Ten times as much effort as it should take! Can you afford such a waste of energy? Why not conserve it—for more purposeful use?

Reducing muscular tension has a powerful effect on your emotional life. Poise of body—as Yoga and Zen exponents know so well—is a preliminary step towards poise of mind. They are twin aspects of one quality.

That sense of apathy

When you are filled with a sense of apathy and indifference, you begin the almost frantic search for new pleasures and excitements. When you get them and you find they aren't half as satisfying as you had expected, *the fault is in you, not in the world around you.*

The sunset is still beautiful—if you can be bothered to *see* it. All the things which thrilled you before—they're unchanged. Only you have changed—in that you've lost the capacity to enjoy them!

If you want to get back to a full sense of being alive,

attend to your bodily well-being. Start by making improvements in your physical condition and you'll be taking the first step towards tilting your entire personality back to a state of alertness and balance.

Personality is no ghost

It is no spirit lingering mysteriously in the flesh, blood and bone which is your body. Personality *is* that flesh and blood, as well as the capacity and performance of your brain. It is *all* of you!

Bodily poise shows confidence. When a man is sure of his identity, his place in the world—you can see it in the way he walks, sits, speaks. He puts his feet down surely, knowing that the ground on which he places them is firm.

People recognize that self-sureness. The upright carriage, the relaxed yet perfectly controlled movements —they're as plain to see as the smile on a face. And they aren't simply physical attributes which you have or have not got, like red hair, blue eyes or big ears. *They are the outward, recognizable signs of body and mind in harmony.*

Letting go . . .

Take a man who normally walks badly, put him under hypnosis and tell him to cross the room: hey presto, his posture corrects itself!

Magic? No such thing. The anxiety and tension which usually cramps his muscles has been removed by hypnotism—so his back straightens and his chin is raised.

Have you noticed how when you go to bed at night it can take a long time to get comfortable—yet in the morning, after a relaxing sleep, you're happily at rest in almost any position?

That is the difference which being fully relaxed makes. Simply to lie down isn't to relax. You have to let every muscle go, every part of you. To relax the body, you have to relax the mind—they're too closely connected for one to relax while the other remains tense.

Easier said than done? Well, certainly. We all have worries, and when we lie down at the end of the day they came crowding in, making relaxation almost impossible. You can't just flop down and 'let go' if your worries won't *let* you go.

You need some way to combat this situation. Some way to drive the worries out, soothe your mind into a state of relaxation. To achieve enough control to be able to 'switch off'. And there *is* a way . . .

Controlled breathing

You're horizontal. But you're still restless. Tense.

Take ten or twelve long, deep breaths. Each time, inhale as slowly as you can: count unhurriedly to eight while you're drawing in that breath. With your lungs filled, hold your breath while you count four at the same easy rate.

At first you'll find you want to take quicker breaths. With practice, though, they'll get *longer*. Don't overstrain—if you keep it up for too long it'll make you dizzy. But while you're taking those deeply controlled breaths, think about what's happening. How the air is being drawn into your nostrils, down to your lungs, through the blood-cells to the extremities of your body: then, as you exhale, of the waste product being vented, clearing your system for the next intake of oxygen.

This slow-breathing technique can act as your built-in tranquillizer. Concentrating your thoughts on its regularity and rhythm gradually excludes external worries. As you begin to relax, you sink into the present, into the simple reality of mind and body immersed in its own existence . . .

Now to relax

Deep breathing is only a preparation, readying you for further stages of relaxation.

You're flat on your back. No pillow—better to be completely horizonal. Breathe gently now, easily . . .

Close your eyes. If you're staring at something, you can't be relaxed. Relax your eye muscles and those at the corners of your mouth. Relax all the muscles in your face, forehead, neck.

Direct your consciousness, like a camera close-up, to your arms and shoulders. Consider each inch of them, passing on only when you're satisfied that the relaxation there is total. There's no hurry.

Legs, thighs, ankles, calves, feet. Limp. Toes limp too. If your brow isn't smooth or your jaw isn't loose, you aren't relaxed yet. Don't try to rush it. *Relax—inch by inch* . . .

Total relaxation

This won't be achieved without a lot of practice. But don't let that depress you or put you off making the effort, because even when you achieve only 50 per cent or 75 per cent relaxation you draw considerable dividends from it. *And* you'll be getting better at it all the time. When you relax, you're storing vitality, building reserves of strength and energy, sharpening the edge of consciousness and self-awareness. By giving your body the benefit of complete relaxation, you are removing strains from your mind. Your brain, if freed from worries, will be better able to deal with the things which cause them.

You become yourself: an entity, mind-plus-body. You're swimming with the current of life, instead of trying to swim against it.

Meditation

Relaxation, and the ability to empty the mind of worries which are irritants, enables you to concentrate when you want to on any area or subject of your choice.

On yourself, for instance.

You can call it meditation or you can call it self-analysis, but you'll notice that in these few lines we're back almost to where we started: to the precept *know yourself*.

You can know yourself only by deliberately and systematically thinking about yourself. Assessing what's good, what's bad, what's getting better or worse—what you've done well today, and the things you could have done better . . .

Ask yourself, *What kind of person am I? What am I aiming for? What am I achieving? Am I going about it in the best way available to me?*

(*a*) Whatever ailments you may have, *you* are the best doctor for them.
(*b*) No doctor can expect to cure an ailment until he's diagnosed it.
(*c*) You can't identify a cause until you see it.
(*d*) You won't see it unless you search for it.

So clear your mind of everything but *you*. Examine

and question yourself—and accept only honest answers!

Who am I? How have I changed? Is that good, or bad?

Examine your aims in life, and your progress towards them. Should the targets be extended now? Or reduced?

Think about your friends: the state of your friendships and your contribution to them. Could you play a greater part in them than you do? Don't exclude your marriage, which is a particular kind of friendship.

Think back over what you've done and not done during the day or week. Consider all the areas of your life—business, social, family, etc. Take note of the failures, then forget them. Above all take note of your successes, and see how you can make the most of them.

There's plenty of time. Don't rush it. When you've finished, your mind will be much more clear. Then you can sleep—in peace . . .

(1) Do you regard yourself as considerate in your dealings with others?
(2) Have you any evidence that others regard you as considerate?
(3) Do you think you're fairly clever?
(4) Do you think you're more clever than most of your friends?
(5) Do they know you think so?
(6) Do you listen attentively to others when they talk about things of interest to them?
(7) Or do you mostly wait for *your* chance to speak?
(8) Do you know what you want to say before you start talking?
(9) When someone's left tongue-tied or otherwise embarrassed, do you take advantage of the situation —or try to help them out?
(10) To get your point of view accepted, do you ignore those of other people?

CHAPTER SIXTEEN

'FAILURE' AND 'SUCCESS'

Remember there is nothing stable in human affairs; therefore avoid undue elation in prosperity, or undue depression in adversity.

SOCRATES (469–399 B.C.)

A man I know is a writer. He earns enough to keep his family fed, clothed and sheltered, but that's about as far as it goes. It's a hand-to-mouth existence, and the lack of long-term security—the monthly pay-cheque and the insurance and pension schemes which those in 'regular' employment enjoy—is sometimes enough to cause a sleepless night.

Now this writer has a friend who is a tycoon, chairman of several companies and, by any standards, very well off. He was talking about a new multi-million pound company he was forming, and the writer commented: 'What an exciting life you lead. I envy you.'

The tycoon looked amazed, and replied: 'But I envy *you*!'

The grass is always greener on the other side. The writer envies the tycoon his financial security, power, involvement in the dynamism of current big-business. The tycoon envies the writer his freedom, the amount of time he can spend with his family, the absence of the strains and pressures which a business executive faces daily.

So each looks at the other and thinks, 'I'd like to have what *you've* got!'

What's the point of this story? I'll tell you.

They're both *crazy*!

Well, they would be if they really meant what they said. It would mean that instead of each realizing that he has the life he wants and finds fulfilling, he's wasting time in staring enviously over the fence at what only *looks* like greener grass. Instead of allowing themselves to revel in their chosen roles, to live each minute of each day *aware* of self-fulfilment, each thinks enviously of a life in which he would probably be a total flop!

In fact, I'm exaggerating somewhat. Neither the writer nor the tycoon is really wasting much time. They are both busy, intelligent men, and each consciously enjoys his work. Yet it's also a fact that when either stops to think about it, he envies some aspect of the other's life. *Just as a majority of people waste time looking over their shoulders at other people's success—instead of getting on with their own lives and deriving twice the results, twice the satisfaction in the process!*

Success is a personal issue. The successful man or woman is the person who achieves his or her own goal. It's pointless to think, 'He's made more money, therefore I'm a failure'. It's not only pointless, it's *ridiculous*.

Other people's targets are their own, and their triumphs are their own. You'll only achieve *your* success by sticking to *your* targets! *You can make millions—and be an all-round failure.*

This is a most important point which I must emphasize—because in our ultra-materialistic society it is conventional to equate wealth with success.

The acquisition of wealth is no proof of success. You are not 'a success'—as a person—simply because you've piled up a stack of loot. Nor because you're a record-breaking salesman. In those cases it would be true to say that *you have been successful in making money* or that *you are a successful salesman*. It does *not* follow that you are a successful human being.

As I said in the first chapter, this is not a how-to-get-rich-quick book. I suppose you could call it a how-to-get-the-most-out-of-living book. What's the point of dying rich and miserable? Everything Midas touched turned to gold, but did it make him happy?

Of course it didn't. By all means work hard to get rich—if it will serve the positive purpose of leading to a fuller, more satisfying life. On the other hand it has been proved a million times over that the pursuit of wealth as an end in itself is no route to happiness.

A pattern for success . . .

The target

1. must be an aim which you really want to achieve
2. must be an aim which calls for the full use of your energy and talents
3. must be an aim which you, at full stretch, using those assets to the hilt, are capable of achieving.

Now taking aim . . .

Retain an optimistic view—the outlook of one who is confident he's going to make it because (*a*) he's determined to get there, (*b*) he knows *how* he'll get there, (*c*) he has fortune on his side.

N.B. If you start thinking you *haven't* got fortune on your side, grab her by the ears and haul her along with you! *Because what people are apt to call 'fortune' is more a matter of making and recognizing opportunities than of having them thrust at you.*

Two hundred years ago Richard Sheridan, the Irish playwright, wrote:

The surest way not to fail is to determine to succeed.

On the subject of determination to succeed, remember that a major cause of failure is the day-dream. Instead of saying, 'I intend to become Prime Minister', and then working hard towards realizing that ambition, the day-dreamer *imagines* himself as Prime Minister, then spends so much time pondering on how nice that's going to be that he never even gets nominated for a seat on his local Town Council.

Day-dreaming, however, is quite a different subject from what I'll call

Thinking success

Day-dreaming is escapism, an opiate: the schoolboy, for instance, finds listening to the maths lecture too much like hard work, so he escapes into a private world of dreams. That's one thing; *thinking success* is quite another.

Let's start with an example. Smith and Jones have been summoned to interviews for a new job each particularly wants. How does Smith prepare for it? Well, he gets a good night's sleep, puts on his smartest suit and makes sure he's in the building with at least five minutes to spare before the appointment time. He's going to do his best: he's *hoping* for the best, and when he gets into the interview room he'll 'play it off the cuff'.

Jones has quite a different approach. He sits down quietly and asks himself what kind of man the company is looking for: what experience they're likely to consider important, what characteristics, abilities and attitudes the job requires. He checks carefully how *he* measures up to those standards—the areas where he can score and those where he's less likely to. Now he *imagines* the interview. He imagines the questions they'll fire at him, and he prepares answers to those questions. He imagines himself giving those answers—emphasizing the points which should go down well with the interviewer, skimming more lightly over weaker patches . . . Not only does he imagine the whole interview, but *he imagines it going well. He 'sees' approval in the interviewer's eyes, hears his own succinct, unhesitating answers* . . .

And Jones gets the job. Because he has not only done his homework—he has *thought in terms of success.*

Conversely, if he'd gone in expecting failure, he would probably have failed.

Now take a wider area of operation for the same principle. Jones joins his new company—and he's still *thinking success.* He doesn't think (or say to his wife), '*If* I get promoted . . .'; he thinks (and says), '*When* I get promoted . . .' In effect, he is programming his own brain-computer to produce success—to direct him constantly *towards* success. And he doesn't just 'go through the motions'—he believes in what he's doing. He has so convinced himself that he's on his way up that the company management are soon as convinced as he is!

The fact is this: the brain-computer is as easily programmed by an *imagined* situation as it is by factual experience. An example of this can be seen in demonstrations of what can be achieved under hypnotism. For instance a small, unmuscular man can, under hypnosis, be persuaded to perform feats of strength which, without the influence of hypnosis, would be utterly 'impossible'. The brain has been convinced—by the hypnotist's assurance—that the feat is possible, and so it *becomes* possible.

If you can convince yourself that you can do a thing —you can do it. By conscious exercise of the imagination you can eliminate difficulties and obstacles which in an unimaginative perspective seem insuperable.

But there is no magic in it: the achievement must be within your potential. The weakling who lifts heavy weights when he's hypnotized would never believe, awake, that he had such potential. So awake, he couldn't do it. But the potential is there, to be revealed when his conscious mind, with its barrier of inhibitions, is put to sleep.

Lifting the weight, he doesn't have to groan or grit his teeth, or exert apparently superhuman force. He knows he can do it—because his brain has been convinced of it—so he does it, almost without effort!

And so can you—if you make a habit of *thinking success*.

The fact is that we seldom, if ever, use our full potential either mentally or physically.

Your heart, your lungs—all your organs—hold something in reserve which is there to be called upon at times of real emergency. Ordinarily, in physical terms, most of us use no more than half our full capacity. As an example—a perfectly serious one—imagine a youth competing in his school sports, say in the mile race. He thinks he's putting every ounce of his strength and stamina into it. If you questioned that, he'd think you were crazy—he wants to win, doesn't he? Of *course* he's doing his best!

Now put the same lad down on a race-course, and let a tiger out of its cage behind him. *I guarantee he'll run a lot faster than he did at the school sports* . . .

So you too can be your own hypnotist! Seriously —you *can*. But you must know roughly your own capabilities: that realistic self-image, remember? And you must remember that hypnotism, including auto-hypnotism will work only when the suggestion is (*a*) believed, and (*b*) not in conflict with your own true nature.

'Circumstances' and 'luck' play their part in all human affairs, but they average-out fairly evenly in the long run. 'Good luck' is useless unless you take advantage of it. 'Bad luck' isn't fatal if you can face up to it and deal with it. The man who misses the chances which come his way, or who is floored by every mischance, won't hit his targets—he'll be too busy bemoaning his 'bad luck'.

Some time ago Henry Cooper, heavyweight boxing champion of Europe, found himself in an Italian boxing ring against an opponent who repeatedly fouled him with blows below the belt. The crowd weren't standing for any interference with their hero's tactics, and the referee seemed indisposed to spoil the Roman holiday. Did Cooper surrender to 'circumstances' or 'bad luck'? The hell he did. He pulled one of the best punches of his career out of the bag, and ended the fight in the one way which not even fruit-throwing Italian fans could dispute.

Every one of us is in some way and at some time in a boxing ring. When the fight's going against you, you can either throw in the towel, or produce just that little extra something to swing the tide the other way. It's not up to 'luck'—it's up to *you*! You can profit out of failure. In fact, you *must* make use of it.

William Whewell, born in England in the last years of the eighteenth century, wrote:

Every failure should be a step to success: every detection of what is false should direct us towards what is true; and every trial should exhaust some form of error.

Come to think of it, a much more recent quotation comes from the film of *Chitty Chitty Bang Bang* which has a song with the chorus line 'From the ashes of old failure grow the roses of success'. A pleasant, catchy tune, and—not for the first time—a spark of wisdom in a fairy tale.

Each time you encounter failure, *learn* from it. You're less likely then to fail again for the same reasons. Check back on the methods you've been using; ask yourself 'Am I going about this the right way? Where did I go wrong? Should I rethink my approach altogether?'

Failure can do you a power of good. It can be the challenge which triggers the dynamic will to win! If you win too many battles too easily, you are less likely to stand up to defeat when you encounter it. Learn to make friends with failure—in order to move faster towards success.

We mentioned a fairy story just now. Well, it reminds me that in Thackeray's *The Rose and the Ring* there is a moment when Fairy Blackstick exclaims:

> The best thing I can wish you, my child, is a little misfortune!

Don't let success go to your head

Supposing you've got to the top of the tree? Supposing you were *born* with most of the abilities which enabled you to get there? The smallest chemical difference in one of your glands could have made you a moron instead of an intelligent person. *You* didn't have anything to do with that—you had it when you came into the world—free! So what have you got to crow about?

In Canterbury Cathedral is the tomb of Archbishop Chichele, the founder of All Souls College, Oxford. A man of vast intellectual achievement and great fame even in his own lifetime, Chichele was determined to remember—and remind others—that under the pomp and panoply of wordly success a man remains no more than a man—frail, fallible, flesh and blood. So he had his tomb constructed in two layers. On top, you see an effigy of the Archbishop in all his robes and dignity: below, that of a rather skinny old man, helpless and pathetic in his nakedness.

Might it not be a salutary experience for the great ones of this world—particularly politicians—to have to make one public speech each year in their birthday suits?

Apart from the fact that pomposity is downright silly, remember this as well: whether you're an industrialist, Trade Union leader, prince, politician or public librarian—*whatever* your function or position, you almost certainly look less important to the rest of the world than you may feel yourself to be.

Let the other man know you rate him highly. If you think a great deal of yourself, keep it to yourself!

When things aren't going too well, you may find it helps to put a proud face on the 'image' you're projecting.

This is legitimate—although in general I go along with the Biblical character who said:

He that hath a proud look and a high stomach, I will not suffer him . . .

Putting a good face on things can help, for by displaying confidence you acquire more of it than you're actually feeling. That's good for your morale and as an encouragement towards the sense of optimistic purpose we've already discussed. What's more, it can produce helpful reactions from other people: for by and large they accept the image you present to them.

There is a saying, 'Nothing succeeds like success'. Often what *looks* successful *becomes* successful.

But remember—you're doing it for a purpose. Make sure you can remove the mask and *be yourself* when you wish to. Don't lose sight of what's inside that mask!

And remember this too: *it's when we've reached our targets, when we've become successful and everyone can see it, that we can most afford to be modest.*

As I've already mentioned, there is a tendency nowadays to equate success with money. We live in a materialistic and acquisitive society: we value 'status', and we are conscious of the fact that the Jones's think more of us if we have two cars than they do if we have only one.

Ask yourself this question:

Am I out to achieve what I myself want to achieve—or what the Jones's will respect me for achieving?

You might think it out like this . . .

(*a*) What Jones will respect in me is the achievement he would like for himself.

(*b*) What I need in order to get maximum satisfaction from my life is what will satisfy (=fulfil) *me*.

(*c*) Jones presumably has his targets: I certainly have mine. Jones and I are different people. Why should either wish to ape the other?

And take note, please, of this . . .

If you try to be someone other than yourself, you are trying to hide from your own self-image. You are admitting to feelings of inadequacy: reaching for a disguise, a camouflage under which to shelter. 'Prestige' and 'status symbols'—all of this modern paraphernalia amounts to no more than the deliberate creation of false images.

In earlier chapters I've gone into the necessity for establishing a realistic self-image. The reverse side of the coin is the false self-image. Suppose you convince yourself that this is a true one. Only your conscious mind will be convinced. At deeper levels, in the unconscious mind, you know the truth. It's there, implanted, and you can't excise it. And when the false image comes face to face with the true one—well, did you ever see two fast cars meet head-on? Imagine that happening inside your brain . . .

I've been talking a great deal about success, but comparatively little about failure. To some extent this may be because I have absorbed my own precept—and Sheridan's—that success comes more readily to those who think in terms of it. If you persistently think in terms of failure, you're conditioning yourself to fail.

Do you think *you're* a failure?

If you do, take a sheet of paper, draw a line down the middle, put a plus sign to the left and a minus to the right. Then list under the plus what you've got that you're glad of: not just possessions, but health, family, friends, interests, hopes, expectations—everything that pleases you. On the other side, list the unsatisfactory elements in your life.

Think carefully, take your time about it, and list *everything*. Then check the sum of one list against the sum of the other. The balance may surprise you!

Now on the minus side—whether or not you still consider yourself a failure—take each item in turn and think hard about it. See if there isn't something you can do, or stop doing, to eliminate it altogether. If not to eliminate it, at least to make it less bad, less obviously a 'minus' on the score-card.

Don't just mope over those minuses and feel sorry for yourself! Problems usually seem much bigger than they are—until you tackle them realistically.

135

That's why making a list of pluses and minuses on paper, then sorting out each problem for separate attention, is much more than a gimmick. When you're in a state to be thinking about failure, the negative side looms larger than life-size. Little irritations, become major problems. Linking them together, you find what looks like a sea of troubles. But when you've separated them and pinned them down for close examination and treatment, you begin to regain perspective. To get back into balance . . .

And then you must act—instead of only moaning!

The green-eyed monster

Do you ever feel jealous, envious of another person's success? In a way, worse off yourself because he's become better off?

You probably won't admit it, because you know that envy and jealousy are not laudable emotions. But between you and me, I'd guess there must be occasions when the only honest answer would be 'yes'. Let's look at an example.

Jones has become a director of his company. He and his wife were friends of yours. There's little chance of your getting that kind of promotion in *your* firm, and you and your wife are well aware of it. So Jones's success has suddenly made you feel like a failure.

What's more, Mr. and Mrs. Jones have changed. They're moving in new social circles, they have a luxurious new car, and—well, success has gone to their heads, and it's driven a wedge between you.

Now hold on a minute!

I wonder if you aren't blaming the Jones's for a situation which is largely of *your* making . . .

Point one: Jones has a new car. Do you imagine he got it in order to annoy *you*?

Point two: he's been promoted. So his social life, which naturally is to some extent tied up with business, blossoms into new areas. You can't put more than a pint into a pint mug, so it follows that the Jones's will have less time to spend with their old friends. They've got to see these new people—that doesn't mean they're *choosing* to ignore *you*.

But if you and your wife have been resenting this situation, it's likely that the resentment has been noticed. So where did the wedge come from? From Jones, or from you?

Only you can answer that question. But let me put another thought in your mind. Jones was—potentially still is—a friend of yours. One of the benefits of friendship is that friends help one another. Jones is meeting new people—more influential people.

It sounds as if you could use a bit of influence. Isn't this a crazy time to let a friendship fall to pieces?

Anyway, who says he's better off?

Jealousy is such a stupid emotion.

Your neighbour has a bigger car, a bigger house, he wears more expensive suits, and—but that's enough to indicate that his material possessions out-match yours. He looks so much more successful . . .

So you're jealous of him?

Does he have a more successful marriage? Do his children love him as yours love you? For all his money and possessions, *is he a happier man than you*?

That's what counts. Come to think of it, it's possible that the strains and stresses of that high-powered job are turning him into a nervous wreck.

Who says he'll die happy? Who says you won't?

I was telling you earlier how to set about relaxing, and how to set yourself—in a state of physical relaxation —to meditate. I suggest this as a regular physical and mental exercise. Do it every day, if you can spare the time—if you can't, once a week is better than not at all. But do it *regularly*, because it is an exercise you need to practise if you're going to do it properly.

And now that I've given you some ideas about *thinking success*, I want to run the two exercises together and invite you to:

(1) Relax completely (see page 121).
(2) Release your mind into calm meditation.
(3) Mentally *act* success.

I'm not suggesting you day-dream. I'm proposing that you deliberately envisage one area of your waking life (office, home, or an area in which you are normally active and interested) and imagine yourself at work, in conversation, doing whatever it is you have to do or would like to do. In all the imagined actions, in all the words you 'put into your own mouth', follow the precepts recommended in this book. When you find you've gone wrong, stop and correct yourself. Then start again. Direct your words and actions, in your imagination, towards achieving the results you would like to achieve—*towards success*. Direct yourself (the image of yourself) as a film director directs a star on the set.

By rehearsing the part, you'll learn to play it properly when it's 'for real'. By mentally practising the precepts given in these pages, you'll train yourself to use them in your real, everyday life.

(1) Are you particularly anxious to 'create a good impression'?

(2) Do you tend to judge others by the way they dress?

(3) Are you more concerned with the way you look than with the way you behave?

(4) Are you easily put off by someone you 'don't like the look of'?

(5) Would you be very embarrassed if refused admission to a restaurant because of being unsuitably dressed?

(6) Are you frequently envious of other people's looks?

(7) Do you find it easy to put your imagination to work?

(8) Do you indulge much in fantasy and make-believe?

(9) If so, do your fantasies always work in your favour?

(10) Are you envious of those who are self-assured and self-confident?

CHAPTER SEVENTEEN

ROAD HAZARDS

Skipping, for the moment, the snags *along the way* to success, let's consider the biggest booby-trap of them all: the one that's waiting for you when you get there!

Sneaky, isn't it? I mean, you don't expect it, right in the moment of success. Rather like a soldier being shot by a sniper after the battle's finished . . .

You've worked hard to achieve your chosen goal. Now suddenly you've reached it; like a runner at the end of a gruelling race, you flop down, exhausted.

As your brain steadies and strength gradually returns to your muscles, you look around and realize that it's no dream—it's *true*, you've won! The long, hard slog is over: you've arrived, on that summit in the sun!

Now watch it! Because this is the moment—or it can be —when the trap is sprung.

For years you've had your eyes on a certain goal and all your energies have been directed towards it. The effort has been totally absorbing: you've been at full strength, extending your powers and capabilities to the limit. (Which is right and proper. That's the kind of goal you *should* have—one that demands every ounce of talent you possess.)

But now you're here—and—well, that's *it*. The running's over, the cheers have died away, and everyone's gone home. The light is fading, you're all alone. Now the sun's gone down, the air's a little cold as you make your way slowly from the field. You're not tired any more, you've got your breath back and you know you've won—*Hold it there!*

You've just said those words—*I've won!*

And it didn't thrill you. For years you've dreamed of this moment, and now it's here and the prize is in your hands and already *there is no excitement, no satisfaction in it.*

Why? What's gone wrong?

Well, it's over and done with. You were busy getting here, coping with difficulties, hazards, opposition —forcing out that last ounce of effort. For years it's been a full-time, wholly absorbing preoccupation. Now you've succeeded, and the chapter's closed.

And what now?

Nothing. Literally, nothing. Except a feeling of emptiness and let-down. And the question stirring in your mind: was *this* worth all *that* effort?

You didn't hear the trap spring—but you're in it!

How to stay out of it

Two ways—and you'll need to pay attention to both . . .

(1) *You can't be happy and self-fulfilling, without a positive goal in mind.*

When one target is knocked down, another must be set up in its place. So you must never allow one ambition to become the be-all and end-all. You must remember that—as in outer space—*there is always another place to go.*

Do I hear someone say, 'That's all very well for tycoons, business people, actors, professionals, *young* people . . .'?

But the truth is—it's all very well for *you*, too!

Perhaps you're a widow living on your old-age pension in a boarding house in Worthing. You're rejecting what I've said on the grounds that you can't see what achievement remains open to you in your situation.

Perhaps, you're considering the word 'achievement' in too narrow a sense. For instance, if you play bridge, you could study the game and make yourself a better player. If you value your friends, you can develop your friendships and start new ones too. If you lack friends, you can set out to make some. What hobbies and interests have you discarded? Couldn't you take fresh interest in at least one of them? It needn't be expensive, many opportunities are free.

Whoever you are, you must never be without a goal. When one target is down, put up another!

(2) *Dedication to an ambition can be the driving impulse in your life—but it can't be life itself.*

If you allow the achievement of your goal to become all you think about, to possess you utterly, don't be surprised if, when you reach it, there doesn't seem much left that interests you.

But if you've remained in touch with life as a whole —with people, friends, family and all the other interests open to you—then *reaching your goal is only completing a stage in one area of your life.*

It may be a most vital area. But however satisfactory the achievement—even if it's a major triumph—it's still only one strand in the skein of what you are.

Although you must have goals and pursue them, life is not a race in the sense of running flat-out with eyes for nothing but the winning-post. There are pleasures and fulfilments all along the way. So—*aim for the future, but for heaven's sake live in the present!*

Each day is one small section of your life. Each day, each hour, each minute is a precious gift you can use or waste—enjoy, or let go almost unnoticed. Imagine a doctor has just told you that you have only ten days to live. Won't each day count as much as any previous year? Won't each hour matter as much as any month you've squandered in the past? You know as well as I do—the time will come when you *do* have only ten days to live. So why not start *now* and get full value from each day?

We have to *use the past*—in order to learn from our our failures and successes.

We must *aim for the future*—where we've set our targets.

We can only *live in the present—because that's where the living is!*

What do you mean, *you can't*?

One of the biggest handicaps with which people burden themselves is *lack of confidence*. And it is, as often as not, people who *burden themselves*: it is they who, as a result of their own delusions, deprive themselves of confidence.

You may have noticed that in discussing meditation, I wrote:

Take note of the failures, then discard them. Take note of the successes too, and see how you can build on them for the future.

The words I want you to note are 'then discard them'. Look back to chapter 16 (page 131) where I quoted William Whewell's words, 'Every failure should be a step towards success'. In other words, you must *make use of failures.*

If you don't, you waste the experience of it—and the chances are that you'll repeat a mistake where you should have 'learnt your lesson'. Obviously you can't *retain an optimistic view* if you *dwell on* failure. That's why you should first use it, then discard it.

Confidence and optimism run together, and you need both. But you can't feel confident *or* optimistic while constantly reminding yourself of past mistakes. You *can* if you concentrate on past successes!

This is positive thinking and commonsense. If you fill your mind with failure, you gear yourself to fail. If you concentrate on success, you'll expect success and you'll stand a good chance of getting it.

When you recognize self-doubt

Set yourself deliberately to remember your old triumphs. Things you felt proud of at the time. The days you 'won' and were acclaimed for it: the more personal successes which perhaps only you knew about. The 'concrete' achievements, and the emotional ones. The human relationships you handled well enough to bring real satisfaction.

Turn your mind back to those days and moments when you heard, however privately, the cheers and trumpets. Bask in them—it's a pleasant way of passing a few moments! Draw into the nostrils of your memory that old 'sweet smell of success'—and determine now that you'll smell it again—and again . . .

Still doubt if you can win?

Of course, it's possible you're right. This could be one of those targets which is out of your range and which therefore shouldn't be attempted. But don't give up too easily. It may not be out of range at all—it may only look as if it is.

First, put your memory to work. Think of some previous occasion when a project terrified you yet later proved to be well within your scope. In *this* particular case:

(*a*) Do your prospects look worse than they did on that occasion?

(*b*) Might you not achieve a similar success?

Second, ask yourself:

(*c*) What is the basic practical difficulty?

(*d*) Is there some way in which I can overcome it/by-pass it?

(*e*) If the answer is 'yes'—go ahead! If it's 'no'—

(*f*) Where can I go?/How can I learn?/Whom can I ask?/What can I do?/—to acquire the ability, know-how or assistance which I need to overcome the problem?

If there's a positive answer—use it. If there isn't, well, at least you've tried. And you won't look back in five years' time and blame yourself for having let an opportunity slip.

Self-conscious, are you?

Do you feel awkward when you walk into a crowded room? Self-consciousness, of course, springs from lack of confidence, but before we go on, let's be sure you understand the difference between *self-consciousness* and *self-awareness*.

Self-awareness is knowledge and understanding of ourselves, it is *the* essential tool in the business of living and relating our personalities to those of others. *Know thyself:* the words were carved on the temple of the

Delphic oracle, in ancient Greece. As I've pointed out earlier, you can't establish your personal targets, the course and pattern of your life, *without* knowing yourself, what you are and what are your capabilities. Nor can you hope to understand others without first understanding yourself, the personality which is the 'window' through which you see them. That's what we mean by *self-awareness*.

Now *self-consciousness* isn't the same thing at all. The person who is self-conscious isn't *aware of himself*: he's *aware of other people's awareness of him*. He imagines himself as he thinks he looks in their eyes, and the image is invariably unflattering. So he blushes, stammers, fidgets, fingers his tie—goes to considerable lengths, in fact, to make himself look like some kind of idiot.

So it isn't how people see you, that makes you act so strangely. It's how you *think* they see you. The trouble is entirely in your mind, and it is in your power to eradicate it! Let's see how . . .

First of all, by cultivating self-awareness. Knowing yourself is three-quarters of the way to being unworried by what another person may *think* of you. It's the broad, sure basis for absence of self-consciousness—which is the same thing as saying *for poise*.

But while you're working towards lack of self-consciousness, here are a few practical thoughts on fighting the symptoms when you feel them stirring . . .

1. Relax

Let go. Don't try to stand, walk, sit, talk as you think you ought to stand, sit, etc. Don't picture yourself doing it—just *do* it! Don't at once start worrying that perhaps it wasn't a clever thing to say—it's said, so forget it. Who's asking you to be clever, anyway?

Try to imagine you're alone—or that the strangers whom you're facing are your closest friends. Then you can be natural, you can be *yourself*. You have only to adopt such a pretence for a little while, and you will find the battle's won.

'Letting go' is the key, and here's an example of how it works . . .

If you take a wooden plank, say about six inches wide, and lay it on flat ground, you'll find no difficulty in walking from one end to the other. As long as you're reasonably sober, you won't even consider the likelihood of slipping off.

Now find a brick wall twenty feet high and the same width as that plank, and try walking along it. Not so easy, is it? In reality there's no difference—but you're scared of falling, and it's that which makes the difference! You sway and falter—through sheer fear of falling, you fall.

The wall is the same width as the plank. The difference is in your mind and nowhere else. When it's a plank on the ground you can stay on it for hours without stepping off: when it's a high wall your imagination says you're doing something dangerous and difficult. If when on the wall you could be hypnotized or otherwise convinced that the plank was still on the ground, there would be no difficulty.

It's the same in a social situation when you're self-conscious. The only influence which ties you up in knots is your imagination. If you realize this and act on it, you'll find immediate improvement.

2. Try looking at *them*

A group of people you haven't met before are staring at you . . .

Does that feel like some kind of nightmare?

Actually, those people aren't conscious of being a group, a corporate multi-eyed body linked in critical study of you. Each of those pairs of eyes belong to an individual, a person on his own. You don't know him —but he doesn't know you either, so the unfamiliarity is mutual, not one-sided. If you feel awkward —self-conscious—you can take action yourself, immediately, to get rid of any such feelings. How?

By 'taking the offensive'. Instead of worrying about what he/they may be thinking when they look at *you*, make it your affair to think about *them*. Ask questions, show interest, take the social initiative. In doing so, you'll find you're beginning to forget yourself!

You can see directly and immediately this works when you study the difference in technique between men who are (*a*) successful, or (*b*) unsuccessful (= shy) in their relationships with women. The shy lad is concerned to know how the girl will react to him. He shows his embarrassment, his over-eagerness to please, his sense of disappointment when her reaction is less than enthusiastic. He is, in fact, self-conscious—and he gets nowhere very quickly. Now the other man, who is not self-conscious or nervous, steps up with an entirely different attitude. His view is outward, *towards* the girl: he ignores the question of whether or not she likes the look of *him*, and goes all out to let her know he's extremely interested in *her*! He makes so much of his interest in her that you might imagine he doesn't care whether she likes him or not. In fact, he cares as much as anyone else does. But he has the insight and/or experience to know that what will make the girl interested in him *is his interest in her*.

Well, this isn't an instruction manual for those who wish to 'chat-up birds'. I've only given you an example of the advantages of an unselfconscious attitude in human relationships.

Courage!

Even to use the abilities which you know you possess, *en route* to your chosen goals, you need a spot of courage. It's so easy to decide not to risk failure, by not trying to succeed. Or to avoid decision by delay, procrastination, and telling yourself, 'There's plenty of time. Next week will do . . .'

Problems nearly always look tougher than they are —until you tackle them. *When something which worries you looms in the horizon, go out and meet it half way.*

You'll find (*a*) it's less frightening at close quarters, (*b*) it's easier to deal with on your own positive initiative than if you wait for it to come knocking on the door, (*c*) there is great personal satisfaction to be obtained from deliberately facing trouble—and drawing its fangs—instead of trying to hide from it.

We've all had that 'butterflies in the stomach' feeling before, for example, an athletic contest or an examination. And I think most of us have found that the feeling vanishes when action starts. In other words, the best way of not letting the dragon frighten you is to get to grips with it.

Soldiers, sailors and airmen have found the same thing: once in action there's no *time* to be frightened. And while on this subject, one final point. Traditionally, courage is synonymous with battle, heroics, deeds of daring, gallantry, and so on. But this is not the only kind of courage; courage *needs* no battlefield. It is—or should be—part of the currency of our everyday lives.

The German philosopher Johann Richter observed, in about the year 1800:

The grandest of heroic deeds are those which are performed within four walls and in domestic privacy!

Worried?

Some people keep themselves permanently sick with worry. In so doing, they achieve precisely nothing —beyond adding to the worries! Look at it this way:

(1) Either there's something to worry about or there is not.
(2) If there isn't—forget it.
(3) If there is—you can do something about it or you can't.
(4) If there's nothing you can do, you might just as well forget it.
(5) If there *is* something you can do—do it now! If you postpone action for twelve hours, that's sentencing yourself to twelve hours' worry. *Unnecessary* worry.

So—either take action, or put the whole thing out of your mind. But in acting, deal with one worry at a time. If you try to take on too many at once, you'll (*a*) confuse your own brain-computer, (*b*) tend to feel overwhelmed by the collective magnitude of the problems facing you.

Remember how Horatio defended Rome against the Tuscans? He had the sense to make his stand on a narrow bridge across the Tiber—so he faced one man at a time instead of a whole army! That's the way to deal with problems—one by one.

Your brain-computer *can* easily become confused. That author I mentioned at the beginning of chapter 16—he writes novels under two names. Recently he was working out the plot for his next book, and for weeks it refused to 'gel'. Suddenly he realized why. He hadn't decided which of the two 'brands' of novel this one was to be: he had ideas for both, but his brain was hopping from one to the other instead of settling down to one single problem. It was behaving, in fact, like a computer which was wrongly programmed.

Once he realized this, it was easy enough to correct the error. He made a firm decision on which novel he was going to write next, and within twenty-four hours his story-line was on paper.

Commonsense? Well, so it is. But you'd be surprised, perhaps, how many people simultaneously frighten and confuse themselves. They struggle desperately against 'a sea of troubles' when they could take them singly —and knock each one for six!

Action this day . . .

(*a*) You know yourself. This is the starting-point.

(*b*) You know your objective—the target you've set up as a result of that self-knowledge.

The line between (*a*) and (*b*) is the route you have to follow. Your transportation over that route will be faster and smoother when you have adopted the habits of positive living—particularly in relating to other people.

So you have a starting-point, an objective, a route, and what I might call equipment for the journey. At any rate you will have when you've digested all this and learnt to use it as part of your way of life. But there's still one other thing you need: *a self-starter*.

Action is the certain cure for lack of confidence. The one way you can discover whether or not you can accomplish a certain task is to attempt it. The one way *never* to find out is to lack the courage—or the initiative —to move purposefully towards the objective.

It's no good just knowing this and understanding it; you must *use* this knowledge and understanding. Start now—today.

The use of time—full time!

Whether you're 17 or 70, you haven't all that much time that you can afford to waste it. And as I've said, 'knowing' is useless unless it's combined with 'doing'. The French philosopher Jean-Jacques Rousseau wrote:

> To live is not merely to breathe; it is to act; to make use of our organs, senses, faculties—of all those parts of ourselves which give us the feeling of existence.

Thoughts of existence and non-existence pose problems with which the human brain is hardly tuned to grapple. What is true or not true is often based on faith and personal belief rather than on logic and reason. It's a question of your faith or mine, your belief or mine —and who can say which (if either) is right?

But there is one truth of which I am absolutely certain . . . There *is* a life before death!

Occupied with more distant problems, eternity and so on, many of us tend to overlook this unassailable fact. So we fail to make full use of either our full potential or our time. And a loss of time is one kind of loss which nobody can ever truly make up: when a minute is gone, it's gone.

How about trying to use every one of them, starting from now?

(1) Do you accept your habits as unchangeable?

(2) Are you secretly rather proud of them?

(3) Would you change any of them if you could?

(4) Do you ever check over your *thought habits*?

(5) Is it possible that some of your firmest 'convictions' are based on fallacies or wishful thinking?

(6) When you learn a new truth, do you rethink related theories and discard those which are now disproved?

(7) When a truth is unpleasant, do you prefer to ignore it?

(8) Do you attempt to be objective in your judgements?

(9) Are your views consistent? Or do you vary them to suit the occasion?

(10) Do you tend to believe what you're told? Or do you take other people's statements 'with a pinch of salt'?

CHAPTER EIGHTEEN

THE GENERATION GAP

This book is primarily concerned with human relationships—an enormously wide subject. And within its breadth are specific areas which, because they contain problems of their own, need to be looked at separately.

One of those areas is the relationship between parents and children: especially, perhaps, between the middle-aged and the adolescent. I need hardly tell you that it's known nowadays as 'the generation gap'.

You may be a parent already. If you are not, it's odds-on that one day you will be. So if this 'gap' exists, it is a problem which sooner or later faces us all.

Now, I won't deny that the gap *does* exist. But I'll stick my neck out and assert there is no gap that can't be bridged. *There need be no gap, and no problem.*

Like a referee before a boxing match, I will start by addressing each 'corner' separately. First the parents.

Parents—meet your children!

The love your children have for you is either in them or it is not. If it is not, they're missing as much as you are—but it isn't their *fault*. It's not a lack for which you can *blame* them. Love isn't a duty or an obligation: it's a phenomenon!

But children—all new-born creatures—need parental

affection. Lack of it is perhaps the greatest single cause of psychological imbalance. A child must *see* affection, *feel* it, know for sure it's there.

There's a child in *you*

You aren't all adult—not even if you're ninety years of age! You have an adult and a child component in your personality. The child component is sometimes hidden, sometimes very plain to see.

Your possession of this inner child should make it easy for you to understand your children—to appreciate the motivations behind their actions and reactions. You and your children aren't of different species— you're virtually one and the same creature!

For instance, take the point I've just made about children needing love, affection, approval. Don't *you* like to be told how clever you are? Don't *you* want recognition of your virtues, applause for you achievements?

If, sharing as you do so many emotional needs with your children, you can't easily—almost effortlessly —establish a wide and lasting empathy with them in their desires, anxieties and pleasures, you'd better start asking yourself if there isn't something wrong with *you*.

Now let's look at a common example of how things can go wrong between child and parent . . .

Johnny knows his parents love him—and he needs that love. When he's naughty, his mother's attitude changes from love to anger. He can't accept the withdrawal of affection, and his first reaction is to counter parental anger with his own aggression. The average parent resents this, and answers with reciprocal aggression.

('Answered me back, if you please! Stamped his foot

and shouted at me! Well, if I'd done that to *my* mother . . . !')

Now the child knows he's hurt his parents' feelings. And as a result feels guilty. He's 'sorry': and since a sense of guilt is uncomfortable, he learns to avoid setting off the same cycle again by any similar transgression. The system becomes clear to him, i.e.

> Do the right thing = You get love
> Do the wrong thing = You get no love

That's easy for Johnny to understand, so he accepts the code and lives by it. He's still naughty sometimes, of course, and he knows that if he's caught he can expect punishment—or at least a temporary withdrawal of affection. To him this is natural and logical and therefore quite acceptable—it fits the pattern which he is being taught. The child's father, incidentally, is in a similar situation when he drives his car at more than 30 miles an hour in a restricted area—he knows that if he's caught *he'll* incur displeasure, punishment, etc. He knows the penalty and takes the risk. It doesn't make him an outlaw, any more than the child's naughtiness entitles him to be labelled 'bad' or unlovable.

In fact the child will sometimes be testing authority, deliberately checking up on the limits of his parents' affection or permissiveness. If he finds there are no limits, or that his parents don't bother to enforce them, the effect on him can be as harmful as a withdrawal of parental love. Finding no barriers where he expected them, he's as bewildered as if suddenly there were no rail around his play-pen.

You test authority too, sometimes. Your motives are the same as the child's—to see how far you can go. For example—a man is out with his boss for an evening 'off duty'. At some point, he uses his superior's christian name for the first time. No objection is raised: okay, so far so good. Ten minutes later, our friend tries a rather personal joke, a reference to the boss's characteristic behaviour in the office. The great man looks first surprised, then cross; his subordinate thinks, 'Careful. That was going too far.'

But let's get back to Johnny.

Have you ever seen a toddler slip and fall down—and its mother jerk it upright and give it a cuff over the side of the head?

If this happens to Johnny, what goes on in his mind? He's been taught that if he's good, he gets love. That if he's bad, he'll get a smack. Now he's tripped on a polished floor, and his mother has *hit* him for it!

Or perhaps he wet his bed, and was spanked for that. He didn't mean to—and he was asleep at the time. Then his mother or father—who are supposed to love him—cause him bodily pain for something over which he had no control whatsoever!

To punish a child for something he couldn't help is unjust. It can only damage the relationship between you. You can avoid making such a blunder by conscientiously setting out to understand your children's motivations. As I've already said, this requires no great depth of either intellect or insight!

Or perhaps Johnny was lying in his bed one morning and his mother walked in when he was interestedly exploring his own anatomy. That little thing between his legs—he was examining it, fiddling with it. His mother rushes white-faced to his father: then enters father, looking and sounding furious. 'You *dirty* little boy!' More smacks, and a grim silence over breakfast.

(Father is particularly angry, perhaps, because he remembers how frequently he used to play with *his* —and how ashamed *his* parents made him feel.)

157

Now for the child it's all confusion. Confusion, and guilt—no logical reason for the guilt except for the inexplicable parental reaction, but it's still guilt, as uncomfortable and worrying as a sharp stone in the shoe. Guilt, confusion, rejection, insecurity . . . imbalance.

The beginnings of a 'mixed-up kid'. And who mixed him up, for God's sake?

One thing is certain: *he* didn't!

That thing he was playing with—it's his own, isn't it? What is he supposed to do—pretend he doesn't have one? Shouldn't he have a nose either? Shouldn't he touch his left foot? If he does, will he be hit for that, too?

Children are people, too

Your children are not possessions. They're not even pets, like cats and dogs. They're people. They're like you—only of course younger. They're just as entitled as you are to be treated as individuals. They don't have to see things exactly as you see them. Individuals—as we recognized earlier—differ. So their viewpoints and opinions differ too. If you bring yourself to admit that your children are people, you'll find it easier to allow them the right to their views—without resenting the fact they aren't invariably the same as *yours*!

Your 'authority' as a parent is yours because the children need it: they need it because in the early stages of their lives they rely on you for guidance. But the authority is for their benefit, not for yours! They aren't your slaves, nor should you expect them to be scale reproductions of yourself. They need guidance, but not repression: they need encouragement, but not driving: they'll thrive on your love—and return it with interest —but they'll reject absolutely any attempt you make to *possess* them. As they grow older, they'll need less and less guidance from you. It should be a source of pride and happiness to be able to relax the controls, to see the confidence with which they take over their own lives and destinies.

This is what they want, what they need, and it's what you as a parent are *for*!

Sounds like a lot of hard and thankless work?

Nonsense. You'll be repaid a thousand times over —provided you aren't *looking for* repayment—in terms of friendship. *Friendship* is the secret. Not authority, insistence on 'respect', obedience. The basis of successful parent/child relationships is an honest and sincere friendship. From that basis, near-miracles can be achieved. From a basis of 'instructions', nagging, 'laying down the law'—well, it doesn't work in *any* human relationship, and your children are just as much human beings as you are yourself.

Instead of issuing edicts—discuss things with them. Explain your views—and listen to theirs. Don't wait to be asked for help—find out how and when they need it, and *give it*!

Children need guidance: if you like the word better —authority. They need to know there are limits, forms of behaviour which are less acceptable than others, prizes for merit and an absence of prizes (rather than 'punishment') for wrong-doing. But the limits, bounds, must not be arbitrary, established by parental whim —'because I say so!' The laws must be based on reason, and they must be explained and understandable. And as the children grow up, the boundaries must be steadily pushed back: the control is still there, but it's looser, less confining year by year. Until finally they aren't children any more. Then they can make their own rules, build their own fences—and remain your friends!

There are three qualities your children will appreciate in you—*honesty, fairness, feeling*.

Honesty

This is an essential ingredient in all purposeful relationships, and it applies perhaps most of all in your relationships with your children.

You have probably noticed how quickly they see through *dis*honesty. So don't try to fool them. You may succeed at first, but you won't for long, and since the quality of honesty is of primary importance to them in their assessment of any adult, your image in their eyes will be tarnished.

Don't pretend to be infallible. You know you're not God—so do they! So don't *act* God. If you don't know the answer to a question, admit ignorance. If they ask a question which embarrasses you, *admit* to the embarrassment. They'll see it anyway. And when they ask a question and you *do* know the answer, give it to them straight. Don't hedge. *If they want an answer to a question, they're ready to be given it.*

Fairness

I've touched on this already. When you have taught a child to expect a certain reaction to a certain kind of performance, it is grossly *unfair* to react in any different way. The quickest way to shake a child's confidence in you is to let him feel you've treated him unjustly. If he's deserved your censure or criticism, he knows it: if he hasn't, he knows that too. The loudness of your voice won't confuse the issue in his mind—all it will confuse is his trust in you.

When things go wrong in an adult environment—at work, for instance—you may succumb to the temptation to take it out on someone else. In adult circles you can often get away with doing so: partly because an adult recognizes the impulse and the resentment is lessened by that understanding.

But don't expect your children to understand it, Dad. They won't. To them you're being unfair again—lashing out. Do you want you children to think of you as some kind of mad dog?

Feeling

Perhaps the most important quality of all . . .

Children—young people—want to know that their parents (and others) are made of flesh and blood. Love, response, emotion, affection, passion—*feeling*. They want to be close, *feel* close, and they want to know for certain that if you cut yourself it'll be blood and not water that comes out.

So open your arms: relax that 'stiff upper lip'. Waxworks are *out*!

Remember that nowadays neither father nor mother is necessarily right, admirable or lovable.

Simply to be a parent isn't enough. To be respected, you must earn respect. To be loved, you must feel and show love.

What's the difference between the parent/child relationship and any other kind of human reciprocity? Very little. Only that in the early stages the guidance and instruction is all one-way—downwards, from parents to children. As childhood recedes, as children pass through adolescence into adulthood, it becomes a straight relationship between human beings.

If both sides have 'done their bit' it can be the most rewarding experience in your lives.

Keeping in touch

Your children's viewpoints, as I've said, won't necessarily match yours. They may even conflict with them quite dramatically.

Why should this not be so? Are you always so right? When you were a child, did you think exactly as your parents thought?

The rate of expansion of human knowledge has accelerated enormously in recent years. It is still accelerating. As knowledge increases, as man's power within his own world and universe increases, so ideas and thought-patterns must change too. This is precisely what's happening today. *And your children, because they are at school or university, are closer to the roots of new knowledge and new thinking than you can hope to be.*

Isn't it better to understand change, to swim with it, than to resent and fight against it? Even if you want to stop the tide—and I hope for your sake you don't—you won't be able to. No more than Canute could.

If you want to exert any influence on your children, on their ideas or behaviour, join with them in honest, open friendship. You'll get nowhere with a censorious or 'shocked' attitude—that only makes candid discussion impossible.

They don't want censure from you—and it won't help either of you if you try to force it on them. But they *do* want help, advice, support, information, love. You as a parent, as an intelligent and experienced adult, have these things to give—*and you have no right to withhold them!*

You come from a different generation: your experience is not only greater, but different from any experience they will have. Times change, pushed by history, and people change with them. So, as I've said, your views on many things are bound to differ. Consequently, you're going to feel worried and anxious at times. It would be surprising if you didn't!

But—for your sake, and theirs—try to contain that worry. Try to relax. Anxious parents produce anxious children. Anxious children can grow into neurotic adults.

What's the point of spending years raising healthy kids, if when they reach adolescence you're going to turn them into nervous wrecks?

I think that's enough advice to parents. It's time for a word in the ear of the younger set.

Children—meet your parents

If you read the last section, which was addressed to parents, you'll have seen the reference to mothers who wallop their kids for the terrible crime of falling down. You may have wondered, 'How could anybody be so *stupid*? Surely every parent knows better than that!'

Well, let me tell you something: *parents are fallible.*

And here is a thought which you may not find too attractive. When you look at a young mother or father, you can think to yourself, 'There—in a few years' time —is *me.*'

What does this amount to? This: that the fact of being young doesn't make you in any way superior to people of older generations. No more than they are (or were) superior to your grandparents. People are different for all sorts of reasons, and there are areas of difference between generations too: times and climates change, and so do social systems, patterns of behaviour and of thought.

The only way to prove yourselves superior to your parents is by making a better job of being parents—when it's your turn—than they are doing now.

I hope you will—but I rather doubt it. I mean, in broad terms. Because if there was a general tendency for each generation to do better than the one before it, by this stage of evolution we'd all be perfect. I don't suppose I need tell you—we aren't.

The fact that those people are your parents—that they brought you into the world, reared you, taught you, and so on—is no reason for you to be *grateful* to them.

Of course it isn't. They didn't find you, and say, 'We'll take this one and give it life and a home and enough to eat and make sure it passes its "O" levels—to show what nice, kind people we are'. You *happened* to them, that's all—out of a biological process resulting from one unspecifiable mixture of affection, sexual attraction and opportunity. You happened to them, and since then they've performed their role as parents. You've no reason to feel grateful for that—any more than when *you* have a baby you'll expect its first words to be 'Thank you for having me . . .'

But simply to know they are your parents, that you are their child and that without those two particular individuals you would not be *you*, is to *recognize the interdependence which you share with them*.

It is the solid, undeniable reason for a 'special relationship'. For the expectation—or at any rate hope —of shared, reciprocal love and understanding.

I said in the first chapter that you can make the most of yourself only by making the most of your relationships with others. Now that's a fact. And applying it to the subject of you and your parents—here are two people with whom you were born into the closest possible relationship. Here is a gift, in fact—potentially the finest birthday present you'll ever have!

Wouldn't you be crazy not to make the most of it?

164

It's no good just leaving the relationship to look after itself. It won't. It's not automatic—it's like any other human relationship. That gift of the basic, initial closeness which you share—it's fine as a starting-point, but it holds dangers too. For instance—from that degree of intimacy, you can easily expect too much from each other, and be disappointed when you don't get what you expected.

The fact is—and I'm repeating myself quite deliberately—you and your parents are not the same as each other. There may be points of resemblance, but that's about as far as it goes. You'll disagree with some of their convictions, and they're unlikely to go all the way with yours.

So what? Do you—and they—throw up your hands and yell, 'Help, we're different! Look at this awful gap between us!'?

I would like to tell you—in case you didn't know already—that it is quite possible to *love* people without *liking* them. Well, without going quite as far as that, can't you love them and accept the fact that on many questions you and they will not see eye to eye?

You should be able to. And so, of course, should they. If you and they see that this relationship, like all others, needs working at—and if you both not only see it but *do* it—well, what's the problem?

Where's that gap gone?

CHAPTER NINETEEN

DON'T CUT OFF YOUR NOSE TO SPITE YOUR FACE

In chapter 16 we considered the case of a friendship which was ruined when the man whom we called Jones was promoted to the Board of his company. They (Jones and his wife) started moving in different circles, and gradually saw less of their friends, who, probably quite irrationally, felt they were 'giving themselves airs'. And that was the end of *that* friendship.

Now if the resentful one is *you*, what are you (*a*) doing, (*b*) achieving? Well, you're allowing jealousy—the most pointless and senseless emotion in your human repertoire—to spoil a relationship which was formerly an enjoyable one, What's more, you—who are so interested in material gains, status, etc.—are choosing to disrupt the friendship at a time when you could benefit from it. So you're a *double* fool. And what are you achieving? Well, nothing!

In other words, you're cutting off your nose to spite your face.

Jealousy—envy—obstinacy—pride—these are the wreckers of purposeful relationships. And the crazy thing is, they're *avoidable*!

If you're a keen golfer, and every time you lean forward to address the ball you get a twinge of pain in your spine, you'll have the sense to consult a doctor or an osteopath to get the trouble put right. If you're addicted to trivial resentments towards other people

—which we'll equate with the pain in the golfer's back —and you don't take positive steps to eradicate the weakness, you're like the player who does nothing about his pain. He'll suffer—and so will his golf.

(1) Tommy, aged 4

He wants more sugar on his pudding.

MOTHER: It's sweet enough already. Eat it up, now!
TOMMY: Don't *want* pudding, then!
MOTHER: Now don't be a silly boy. Eat your nice pudding.
TOMMY: Shan't!

Result: it *is* a nice pudding, and the kid's hungry, but he doesn't get any because he's too obstinate.

(2) Tommy, aged 40

He expects to succeed to the retiring Managing Director's job. But it goes to his colleague, William. Instead of accepting the situation, Tommy shows his resentment of this 'injustice' on every possible occasion.
Result: before long, he's out on his ear. He's thrown away a good job—because they wouldn't give him a better one!

The child-component in Tommy is still so strong in him at 40 that he reacts to frustration as he did when he was 4. When an emotion stirs him, he surrenders to it —even to his own cost!

Don't think this is such an unusual case-history. It's happening every day—and it might be *you* tomorrow!

As a young doctor in general practice, I worked exceedingly hard. As a matter of fact, I still do. But nowadays I do so more purposefully. If I accept a patient when my time's packed pretty well to the limit,

I do it because I want to help that person and not just because of the fees.

I can still learn *something* from just about *anybody*. If their view is interesting, I'm ready to evaluate it.

In those old days when I was struggling to get to my feet, I had to put up with a lot which today I wouldn't stomach for fifteen seconds.

You have to bend to the wind, at times. You can't afford always to be stiff-necked, insistent on others accepting your advice even if you're certain it's right. You must—within the limits of your convictions—be prepared to compromise.

Today I'd expect some kind of apology or explanation, if for example, a patient failed to keep an appointment without previous notification. After all, it's easy enough to telephone and cancel an appointment. But in those early days, I couldn't afford to stand on my dignity.

I'm not telling this story in order to say, 'Look how level-headed *I* was!" Far from it. I'm telling it as an admission that I was a bit of a fool. Because I *did* allow my pride to show itself—*by not charging for the appointment which the patient had failed to keep.*

That was supposed to be a demonstration of my independence. Actually it demonstrated nothing more than (*a*) pride, (*b*) stupidity. I was fully entitled to the consultation fee. I had a home to keep, and little money with which to do it. What right had I to buy some spurious satisfaction by depriving my dependants?

I was cutting off my nose—and paying for the privilege!

If *you* let *yourself* react in similar ways to minor aggravations—or even big ones!—you are making a slave of yourself. A slave to irrational emotions. You are letting the child within you rule your adult self.

You're behaving like that four-year-old who wouldn't eat his pudding because Mummy didn't put more sugar on it!

The other evening I was dining in a restaurant where the food was absolutely first class, and the price reasonable, so that it was not surprising that every table was taken. A man walked in, asked for a table for two, and was told he would have to wait about ten minutes.

He was furious and behaved like a frustrated child —indeed, he was one. He stamped out—muttering 'ridiculous having to reserve a table in a restaurant like this'.

But the food and service were good. By refusing to wait until there was a table free, he'd done nothing but cut off his nose to spite his face!

Before you spoil a friendship, a useful or potentially useful human relationship, by a display of envy, pride, jealousy, petty resentment or any other form of wilfulness or tantrum, quietly ask yourself these simple questions . . .

(1) Why am I so annoyed?

(2) Am I being logical? Is my reaction an adult one? Could I explain it without feeling silly?

(3) Am I being reasonably objective in my attitude?

(4) If I behave just as my mood dictates, what (*a*) good, (*b*) harm might it do me?

(5) Will my particular behaviour change or remove the source of the annoyance?

(6) Will it serve any purpose, other than air my sense of grievance?

(7) If I exercise self-control and do nothing, will I in the long run have lost anything at all?

Most problems sort themselves out if you decide to think them out. Angry people often forget to think—until it's too late!

BE YOUR OWN ANALYST: 11

(1) Do you sometimes pretend to know more than you do?

(2) Have you any reason to believe you get away with the pretence?

(3) When you don't understand, do you nod vaguely rather than ask for an explanation?

(4) Involved in a conversation in which you know you can't shine, do you (a) move away; (b) change the subject; (c) admit your ignorance and try to learn something new?

(5) Do you feel relaxed and natural (a) at home; (b) at work; (c) at social functions? If not, can you identify the factor/s which inhibit/s you?

(6) What steps can you take to rid yourself of inhibitory influences? (When you've worked it out, *take* them!)

(7) Before an important meeting, do you work out your aims and tactics in advance, or simply 'play it off the cuff'?

(8) By and large would you call yourself a happy person?

(9) If not, what do you think is making you *un*happy?

(10) To achieve happiness—is it up to others, 'luck' and circumstances, or is it in *your* hands?

CHAPTER TWENTY

THE GREAT RAT RACE

The ways of trade are grown selfish to the borders of theft, and subtle to the borders (if not beyond the borders) of fraud. We are all implicated, of course, in this charge . . .

A recent observation? Something to do with take-over manipulations? No, it is another quotation from the writings of Ralph Waldo Emerson. In England, about a hundred years before Emerson in America, George Smollet had been commenting on the corrupting effects of commerce. No doubt we could go back further still—if we wanted more evidence that the 'Rat Race' isn't anything new.

What *is* new is that (*a*) nowadays we are all involved in it, and (*b*) the competition is tougher, more sophisticated and cut-throat than ever before.

Now I see a question in the reader's eyes. Something like 'I thought this book was *not* going to concern itself with commerce?'

You're right—it isn't. That's to say, I am *not* going to tell you how to get rich in six weeks, bankrupt your competitors in twelve or become chairman of your company before you're thirty. If you want to know how to impress the boss with your suitability for promotion, you'll have to look elsewhere.

(*Except that every lesson in human relationships outlined here applies in business as it does in other fields of life.*)

However—as I said in a preamble to chapter 18 on

the generation gap—there are certain areas within the general field of human relationships which present special problems and need special attention. It happens that 'business' occupies a very large slice of the pre-occupations of twentieth-century men and women. For a majority perhaps, it absorbs more time, thought and energy than any other sector of our lives. So I think you'll agree that in the terms of the general discussion we must consider the *effects and dangers* of the Rat Race —what it does to you, how you can live with it and even *in* it and still remain a human being.

The Rat Race is here to stay. If anything, it will absorb us more and more totally during the next decades than it does at present. I believe there are certain attitudes to it which make a lot of the contenders in the race deeply unhappy and dissatisfied. I say 'I believe'—in fact I *know* it, because I meet examples of such malaise every day. Now if I can suggest some new angles or possible approaches, it could prove helpful to some who would otherwise become its victims.

Gather round, rodents . . .

If you can't beat 'em—join 'em

It's a fact that many dislike the commercial life. They live for the end of each day and the train home: for the end of each week, and those two days in the garden. (Or in the car, the boozer, at 'the pictures'. Anything *but* the office or the bench!)

A lot dream about escape. They dream of their private island in the sun: of some form of livelihood in which the daily transport home won't figure.

It's natural enough. A man treks to and from his work, does the best he can, and brings home his pay-packet. By the time essentials such as the interest on the mortgage and the butcher's bill have been settled, there's little left to show for a week's or a month's work. It feels like being on a treadmill: you have to keep moving in order merely to stand still.

I suggest the answer is *not* a change of job which pays a few shillings more. This won't count for much in relation to the weight of the problem we're discussing.

The answer *is* to find a job you can enjoy. Either locate areas of satisfaction in the job you are doing or move to a new one where you can find such satisfaction.

Cold comfort? Well, let's face it.

(1) In order to earn a living, you need a job.

(2) Since you have to, you might as well find one that suits you. Why surrender to misery when you *could* find a little pleasure?

(3) If you can start to enjoy your job, or to enjoy the company of the people with whom you work, or even just *make the effort* to enjoy it, you'll find you're working better too. When this produces its rewards, you'll get the best of both worlds!

The man who has his heart in his work is going to be more successful at it than his colleague who doesn't even try to like it. So—even if you're sceptical—try *pretending* to yourself that you like it. You may end up finding you really do!

Frying pans and fires

We tend to forget that there is always a situation worse than the one we're in. Sometimes we're reminded of it, though, by getting into a worse one—and suddenly realizing that things weren't so bad in the old place, as we thought they were!

So look around for what's good, enjoyable and satisfying in your job. Weigh the good against the bad.

How do you know, if you jump into the fire, that you won't afterwards wish you could climb back into the frying-pan?

'Gamesmanship'

The easiest way to enjoy one's place in the Rat Race is to become imbued with the competitive spirit. To become truly involved in it: a dedicated player.

But how can you reconcile your private ethical standards with the corporate morality—in some cases one might call it corporate *immorality*—which as an 'organization man' you will have to adopt as your standard of behaviour at least five days of the week?

To put it another way: how can you treat your neighbour at home with the decency and respect due from one human being to another—and from Monday to Friday be ready to steal his money and cut his throat?

A little exaggeration, of course. But make no mistake —modern business *is* ruthless, self-seeking and pragmatic. The weak go to the wall, and the strong survive.

So where do you make *your* stand—as a human being lacking the natural instincts of a rat?

I'll give you the answer in two separate parts . . .

(1) *Treat business as a game—as a sport which, like other sports, has its own rules.*

If you're playing rugby football, you'll tackle a member of the opposing team—even if he happens to be your friend—by hurling yourself at his knees and bringing him down as hard as possible. But if you saw him out shopping with his wife on Saturday morning, you wouldn't rush up and knock him down, would you?

Of course not.

As with that rugger match, so with business. Let's say Smith, Jones, White and Green are level-pegging executives in a large firm. They can be friends, know each other socially, *like* each other. (They don't *have* to: see the reference to business friendships, chapter 14.) But however friendly they are at 'real' levels—that is to say *outside the game*—each is out to get promoted, to 'get on' as fast as he can. If Jones can only climb by standing on Green's shoulders—and perhaps by giving him a heel in the teeth at the same time—well, Jones in this game is his own team, and he has a responsibility to his wife and family. He owes it to them that he should progress, earn more and increase his importance in the firm. So Jones has to be ready to take advantage of any progressive opportunity that confronts him, and so has Green—indeed, it's up to each to look after himself.

They all know the rules—or the absence of rules. That's how the game works. If Jones is too 'decent' to seize the opportunity when it presents itself—well, next week it'll be *Green's* heel in *his* teeth.

They wouldn't treat each other like that at home. But that's just the point—they *aren't* at home, are they? They're engaged in the Rat Race Game, where few holds are barred!

Does this sound merciless? It is. But nobody is forced to compete. If Green doesn't feel tough enough to stand the racket, he can bow out and find a job where risks and prizes are smaller. If he can't take the strain of the power game, all he has to do is step out of it. He'll forego the power—but he won't get his throat cut.

And it's 'tit for tat'. We just visualized Jones hurting Green. Now he'll knife Smith, if Smith's in his way and vulnerable to the stab. But Jones must know that Smith might just be smart enough to get in first with *his* knife.

The rules of this 'sport' apply both ways. It's no good shouting 'foul' if it's your back that stops the blade!

(2) *And why not use your devil?*

For the other answer to that question (what chance is there for a non-rat?) let's refer back to a point made in an earlier chapter. Writing about marriage, I said that in each of us there is both angel and devil: that each element seeks expression and that without such an outlet it is difficult to live one's life to the full.

For people with strong 'devils', war and the more aggressive forms of sport can be satisfying outlets. And what sport is more aggressive than the cut and thrust of modern business?

So here's an arena into which you can release your devil—and no need to be ashamed of him either!

It isn't as far-fetched as it may seem at first sight. We all possess different forms of energy, according to motivation, opportunity, etc. If metaphorically speaking, the 'devil' in us is permanently cooped up, the personality can't be an integrated whole: it's incomplete and out of balance. The fullest use is made of our total personality when each part is directed towards the target which it is designed to hit.

Laughable? Jekyll and Hyde—an angel at home and a devil in the office?

I suggest quite seriously that, whether you are aware of it or not, most people who live full, contented lives and who are also materially successful, direct their energies in very much this way.

Never forget you're 'you'

Back to first principles for a moment . . .

You know yourself, who and what you are. But when you're playing the Rat Race Game, you'll be acting a part. Even if you're the Giant Rat himself.

(Well, *one of* the Giant Rats. Judging by what one reads in the financial columns, there must be quite a few about.)

Never forget that behind the rodent-mask is *you*. Inside your brain is the knowledge that *you as yourself* —unlike you the Giant Rat—would never think of employing the methods which you have to use from time to time to avoid being devoured by your fellow rats. Remember that the rules of the Rat Race Game are not your rules as a human being.

Remember too that

(*a*) There is a much wider life outside the Rat Race Game, and that the satisfactions are more worthwhile and lasting than the financial and power rewards *inside* it.

(*b*) There are wider and deeper interests out there, too—and you can retain your involvement in them.

(*c*) Outside the game, human beings aren't just competitors or victims—they're *people*.

(*d*) You're one of them. This is where your *real* life is. The Rat Race isn't real—it's a means towards a purely material end which, in the business of living, is quite a minor issue.

And at this point, in this particular context, some lines I wrote in chapter 17 are so apposite that I'm going to repeat them here . . .

If you allow the achievement of your goal to become all you think about, to possess you utterly, don't be surprised if, when you reach it, there doesn't seem much left that interests you. But if you've remained in touch with life as a whole—with people, friends, family, and all the other interests open to you—then reaching your goal is only completing a stage in one area of your life.

That, of course, is the way it should be. But if you

become so lost in the race that you are deluded into thinking it's real, that it matters as much as life itself —that it *is* life itself—well, one morning you'll go to your shaving-mirror and all you'll see looking back at you will be a—

All right, you've guessed it.

Don't be ashamed to compete

Financial success or lack of it is only one small aspect of the wider business of living purposefully. You aren't 'a success' simply because you're rich, or 'a failure' just because you're hard up.

But don't get the idea that it's unnatural to strive for economic improvement. Why should it be unnatural? We're descended from cave-men, and long before anyone had heard of a 'consumer society' it was the cave-man's job to provide his mate with an adequate shelter in which to live and raise her young. He had to risk his neck getting food, driving off predators, and so on. He also wanted to satisfy himself—and impress his wife —by becoming an important man in the tribal structure.

So what if he *hasn't* changed much in 25,000 years?

The impulse to acquire wealth and power only throws him off the rails when it becomes the sole driving force in his life, and when its achievements—measured in terms of possessions—become the only yardsticks by which to judge 'success'.

Are you 'Ratty' enough?

One final caution . . .

We've discussed the question of setting targets within your range and the importance of avoiding unrealistic goals.

If you're in business, keep this in mind. Perhaps your self-image is big enough to cope with your promotion.

On the other hand, promotion could be more or less automatic, and you might find yourself inadequate to the task. That would be a mistake on the part of your company—for which *you* would suffer.

You might be surprised to learn how frequently this kind of mistake is made. The results vary from stomach ulcers and heart failure to psychiatric disorders of all kinds.

Similarly if you aren't sufficiently aggressive and 'go-getting' to enjoy the ruthless in-fighting which takes place in the corridors of power, you'd be better advised to steer your business career into calmer waters. *Leave competition in the 'Tycoon Stakes' to those who are quicker on their feet—and handier with their knives!*

And now suppose you are as tough as nails: that your footwork is as fast and sure as a champion boxer's. Suppose you have all the attributes of a Rat Race Winner—with one exception . . .

Suppose you have a conscience? Suppose your angel is stronger than your devil: that it would be difficult for you to use your abilities to the detriment of more vulnerable competitors?

Well, don't try. Don't compete. You're probably twice as big as a man, as a human being, as the fellow who will go in there in your place—and win. But you know yourself: you don't have to prove anything to anyone else, do you? So stay out of it.

Elbert Hubbard—I've already quoted him, on another subject—wrote some words which sum up this kind of situation. He said:

To fail to win the approval of one's other self is defeat, and there is none other.

It's the kind of defeat no man can live with. I wouldn't wish it even on a rat.

CHAPTER TWENTY-ONE

THE PRODUCTION LINE

There is another aspect of the business influence which, if allowed to spread unchecked, can achieve nightmarish proportions.

It's the pressure to conform. To *look* like everyone else, *talk* like everyone else, *think* like everyone else.

To become, in fact, the Organization Man—indistinguishable from every other Organization Man.

The drift has been going on, of course, for a long time. You get the 'City Gent' outfit—bowler hat, striped trousers; a striped shirt is usually topped by a plain white collar. Now this character *has* to know the current Test Match score. If by chance he doesn't, some similarly attired 'gent' will give him the raised-eyebrow treatment . . . And this isn't only an area in which British 'tradition' takes a hand—in fact far from it. A friend of mine works for an American business consultancy firm in Britain. He is required to conform to his company's idea of working clothes so closely that it's not very different from being in uniform. Dark suit, black shoes, dark tie, white shirt. *Never* a striped or coloured shirt. No umbrella, and no bowler hat permitted. And there'll be a shocked silence among his colleagues if he doesn't know which teams are playing in the Cup Final. *Now isn't this ludicrous?*

Why an employer should want his employees to look —or be—exactly alike, I simply do not know. Perhaps they're easier to control when they conform so closely to a pattern that their actions and reactions are predictable. Or perhaps he's scared that individuality in dress might lead to individuality in thought. They might one day get some ideas of their own!

But seriously, I think this uniformity is a greater, more insidious danger, and that it threatens you far more than all the obvious dangers implicit in the Rat Race.

I know a man who opted out of business life largely because he couldn't accept the obligation to conform. He'd spent years in one of the Services, and looked forward to the comparative freedom of civilian life. But on shedding one uniform, he found himself being forced into another: and the imposed 'strait jacket' was more than he could stand.

Resisting the pressures

If such pressures have an irksome effect on *you*—and let's face it, they can be enough to drive a sensitive person stark staring mad—the best advice I can give you is:

(1) *Change your job.* If you have the opportunity to move to a company which allows you to remain an individual—grab it!

(2) *Treat it as a joke.* If there is no such escape, then *pretend* to conform. Let the management think you're good zombie material. Inside, remain yourself—and use your sense of humour to give yourself a light perspective of the whole charade.

(3) *Treat it as a game.* If you are secure in the knowledge that when you get home at night you can shed the role with the uniform—if you remain constantly

aware it's a game you're playing—it won't 'get under your skin' as it would if you confused the game with real life.

(4) *Remind yourself that the creature inside the uniform is you—not just an employee, but an individual.*

Hang on to the person you know yourself to be, to your own identity. If there is any motive in exerting pressure on you to conform, it's with the object of forcing you into a mould—*into a standard form* . . .

What a truly horrible thought!

Every human being is unique. Each *has* a machine —a brain—but none of us *is* a machine. There are no two exactly similar human beings in the world. Surely, then, it's a crime against humanity to try to force people to resemble each other?

The goods your company manufactures are no doubt mass-produced. But you weren't. You were custom-built! A unique product—not *better* than the others, but *different*.

It isn't only inside the business organizations where the pressure is exerted. The Press, radio and the television commentators tell us what to believe. Advertisements tell us what to eat, drink, wear, use. Politicians tell us what to think, want, need, hope, accept, reject —and so on.

Now let *me* tell you *this*:

1. The only person who truly knows what you want, what you need, what you think or believe—and so on —is *you*.

2. It is absolutely vital *for you and for society as a whole* that you

   (*a*) remain yourself;
   (*b*) resist attempts to mislead you into false conceptions of yourself or of your needs;

(*c*) refuse to be forced into any mould of someone else's choosing. If your brain needs washing, wash it yourself!

(*d*) retain your own perspective, views and tastes;

(*e*) remain a thinking, discriminating individual. Change your views only when you're convinced —not when you're *told* to!

And why do I implore you to resist these subversive pressures? Here are a few reasons . . .

(i) You can't live purposefully unless you know yourself.

(ii) You can't know yourself if that 'self' can be changed and shaped at someone else's whim.

(iii) You were born a human being and nobody on earth has the right to turn you into some kind of robot.

(iv) This book and every argument in it is aimed at helping you, the individual. The basic principle of *knowing yourself*, then continuing logically towards *knowing and understanding others*, none of this can have any real significance unless you retain your individuality, your personal uniqueness as a human being—and *insist on it*!

If you surrender your individuality, what is left?

Any biologist will tell you that differences between individual specimens of living creatures become smaller, fewer and finally vanish altogether as one traces life back into its lower, more primitive forms. You don't find among worms, for instance, the differences which are so apparent between dogs. The more developed, and more aware and sensitive the creature is, the more it differs from its fellows.

So individuality is one of the distinctions possessed

by the higher forms of life. Humanity is the highest of them all. *Should man surrender what has taken billions of years to develop?*

You are *not* like the man next door. You never will be. You are you, and he is himself, and you can both thank God—or the processes of evolution—for it.

An American, William Channing, wrote 150 years ago:

The great hope of society is individual character.

Make sure therefore that you are not the subject of a 'take-over' bid.

(1) Do you know what your goals are at this moment?
(2) Are you certain they're the right ones for you?
(3) Are you satisfied you're on the right track to reach them?
(4) Are you *certain* you shouldn't rethink your aims?
(5) Granted the targets are the right ones, are you convinced you don't need to run a check on (*a*) route, (*b*) methods?
(6) Are you satisfied with present progress—or should you reconsider your position?
(7) If you're certain of reaching your present goal, should you consider raising your sights *now* —taking that first goal in your stride on the way to one beyond it?
(8) Are you allowing yourself time to enjoy life *en route* to your aims?
(9) Are you making friends along the way—or just using people as stepping-stones?
(10) Imagine what it'll be like when you reach your target. Does the satisfaction of getting there justify the effort you're putting into it now? *Or should you advance on a wider front—achieving broader success in purely human terms?*

CHAPTER TWENTY-TWO

OUT TO GRASS!

That title is like an Aunt Sally set up in order to be knocked down. Because what I'm going to talk about now is *retirement*—and the gist of what I have to say is that retirement should *never* be regarded in the sense of your being 'put out to grass'.

It's just another stage in your life. Part of the pattern of your whole existence. The moment of retirement isn't the end of anything that matters: it shouldn't be felt as the end of your world, because it's no more the end to you as a person than, for example, leaving school was. It's simply one more event in the course of your life.

Think of those rockets being fired into space nowadays. They have what are called 'stages'. The first lifts the whole thing off its launching pad: then the second stage fires, and the first falls away while the main body of the rocket is thrust out of the earth's atmosphere.

Forgive me if my description is technically inaccurate. But could we compare that first stage to childhood and schooldays? The second to your business-career years?

Out in space, the craft sails close to a new orbit. It's finished with those huge powerful motors which drove it out this vast distance, closer and closer to its objective. The motors aren't blasting away any more: but the space-craft is still very much on course, moving steadily towards the culminating success of its mission . . .

As you are, in retirement. You're a human being, not a 'work unit'. You were born to live a full, whole life—not just to serve some limited commercial or professional function, and then call it a day.

You know what a day is—twenty-four hours. Well, it's twenty-four hours before you retire, and it's the same length after that event takes place. And each day in your life is as important as any other. Your life starts when you're born, and ends when you die: there are no other beginnings, no other endings.

The majority of people engage in money-earning activities, roughly speaking from the end of their teens to half-way between sixty and seventy. It just happens that society—and commerce—have organized matters in that way. Why should you regard the end of you money-earning period as some kind of preliminary death?

It isn't. No more than leaving school was. But you can make it so—if you're determined to—by doing nothing after you've retired.

An elderly horse is content with a field of grass, but human beings aren't designed to do nothing. We're born with the instinct and the need to *be*, to *act*, to *live out all our capabilities*.

(*a*) If a muscle isn't used, it becomes useless. It withers.
(*b*) If a hinge isn't moved or oiled, it rusts and becomes stuck.
(*c*) If a brain isn't exercised, its possessor loses powers of thought, reason and imagination.

There is no time in life at which we can afford to stop being ourselves!

And 'being ourselves' means *using* ourselves. It makes no odds whether you're seventeen or seventy, if you're a human being you must continue to act like a human being. *Any attempt to emulate the cabbage will root you as firmly to the ground as any cabbage you ever saw!*

'All very well', you complain. 'But I've been going to the office every working day for nearly fifty years, and now suddenly that's over—what can I do with myself?'

I can't tell you *exactly* what to do, because I don't know your interests. But whatever they are, now is the time to develop them further. It's also a time when you can start new ones.

There are obvious occupations such as gardening and walking. Perhaps you're fond of reading—and if you aren't, why not try it now? What about subjects of particular interest you've always wished you had the time and opportunity to study? Public libraries, museums and most art galleries are free, you know!

There are millions of hobbies open to you. Model-making, painting, stamp-collecting, music—you name it, and you've got the time to do it. That's what you've been given—*time*. It's a commodity which for most of us was in short supply. You can now see it as a gift greater than you first imagined.

Whatever field of activity interests you, you can make yourself more proficient at it. If—figuratively speaking —you're in the Third Division, you can aim to get promoted to the Second. From the Second to the First. And if you're in the top Division—well, what's to stop you making a bid for the Cup?

But let's think about the most rewarding and satisfying hobby of them all . . .

People

When a man or woman retires from the business life it's *people* that he or she misses most. All those people you saw and worked with every day—and perhaps

188

never bothered much about—now you're cut off from them and you're surprised to realize how much you miss the human contacts.

Well, perhaps you *needn't* be cut off from them. If you've turned some into friends, you'll still see them, won't you?

And if you've lived your life up to this juncture as fully as you should, you'll have plenty of other friends too. If you haven't—well, now is the time to start acquiring some.

The greatest enemy of the individual isn't arthritis, thrombosis or athlete's foot. It's loneliness. You can't start too soon to guard against it, to recognize the simple and solid fact that *people need people*. In retirement, you probably need them more than ever—at least, you're more aware of the need for human company, human reciprocity.

So prepare for that need. Start now. The way to start is to follow some of the methods proposed in this book: from beginning to end!

When young, we fill our minds with fantasies and expectations of the future. We 'look forward' to this, that and the other. If we want those things badly enough, we work towards them too: but they fill our heads and they're the stuff our dreams are made of.

When we're older, we look back. We relive our memories, the satisfactions of the past. In old age, satisfying memories are worth a great deal more than gold.

Isn't this about as strong an argument as you could find for living life positively and to the full? For making use of every ounce of your potential? For seizing every favourable opportunity?

Above all, to do these things in the field of human relationships?

We need friends. In old age, we need both friends and memories of friends. We need to be able to remember people we've known—and, in the act of remembering them, *to know that if we had the opportunity to meet them again tomorrow, the meeting would be a mutual pleasure*. We want there to be as few people as possible whom we could *not* meet again with shared pleasure.

Doesn't that give you a few pointers towards the conduct of your human relationships—both before and after retirement?

The life you're living now is the memory you'll live on when ou're old. Make it a memory worth having!

Ask yourself this: how can anyone retire—who hasn't lived?

Now I want to take these thoughts a step further. To put them in relation to the fact that one day you and I will be dead.

Perhaps you're a Christian, rooted firmly and devotedly in that faith. Or a Buddhist, or a Jew. Well, it so happens that I am a Humanist. But while I admit that what I'm going to say is of particular significance for one who thinks as I do, I doubt if it can conflict, in broad essence, with your own beliefs.

As I see it, I shall have an after-life—a 'life after death'—in some other people's memories. Not in many, perhaps; but I'll gladly settle for the hope that in the minds of those closest to me—my children, in particular —there will be memories, thoughts and feelings which in a sense will constitute a kind of continuation.

According to your own faith, you may believe in some other form of life after death, and I don't want to dispute such beliefs: I'd be stupid as well as impertinent if I did. But alongside your personal religious convictions I hope you will allow my contention that each of us can hope to have the sort of after-life I've mentioned.

I only want to suggest to you that whether you have deep religious feelings or none at all, this consideration should be enough to make each one of us think and act very carefully indeed in all our relationships with other people.

The after-taste of our relationships with others is what we'll live on in old age. The same memories will form the most important legacy any one of us can leave behind.

Isn't that sound cause to make the memories good ones?

CHAPTER TWENTY-THREE

INTO THE LIGHT

I'm too lazy to look back and count the times I've stressed the value of self-knowledge. It's the theme of this book, and it keeps cropping up.

Know yourself. Through knowing yourself, learn to know and understand others. From that basis, learn to relate your personality to the personalities of others.

Yes, that's the theme—and I make no apology for repeating it. Advertisers get their 'messages' through by continuous repetition: perhaps I can do the same. But in any case it *has* to be repeated, because in whichever sector of human experience we prospect, we find it turning up again—and again . . .

Which is natural enough. A basic truth is as basic to thought as is rock to the landscape. Anywhere you choose to dig, if you go deep enough it's there.

And at this present stage of man's evolution it is more than ever vital that we should not lose sight of it. It is the guiding beam which, if we follow, leads to the moon, the stars, wherever we want to go next. It is also the key to living in the present age and retaining in its apparent confusion a sense of identity and direction.

Changing values

As I say, I am a Humanist. It follows that if I am to express my views honestly in areas where they converge on matters of religion, I can only do so from a Humanist point of view. It would be dishonest to do otherwise. So I want to apologize in advance in case anything I write in the closing pages of this book offends those whose religious attitudes differ from my own.

Our world is pushing out its frontiers—literally, reaching for the stars.

Recently acquired knowledge has convinced scientists that this human world of ours is not—as we and our forefathers have been led to believe—the all-important centre of the universe. The universe is infinitely bigger and more complex than we thought, and our earth is one very small speck of matter floating in it. Among the thousands of galaxies of stars many are inhabitable—by forms of life as advanced as our own. *Some are likely to be inhabited—and at that, inhabited by thinking, sensitive creatures who may know a great deal more than we do.*

We earthmen and earthwomen are, in fact, rather small beer in cosmic terms—about as important to the universe as is one nest of ants in one corner of your garden in relation to this globe on which we live. So, contrary to everything which you were brought up to believe, we are virtually insignificant.

Does that thought make you feel lost? Purposeless? Does the idea of man not being so supreme a creature jerk the rug from under your feet?

Well, hang on a minute . . .

Our world is also changing its values

We are moving rapidly from a complex of closed societies to becoming one large open society. Into what modern architects call 'open-plan living'.

Barriers are down—or falling. 'Authority' is no longer

accepted without question. No longer do you hear some paternal voice intone, 'This is what you must do' or 'That is what you must believe'—and accept it without question as an edict to be followed. The idols from whom past generations did accept edicts—political, social and religious leaders whose words were law and whose judgements were infallible—are no longer believed in quite the same way. We recognize, now, that they were (and are) men and women like ourselves—just as fallible. Truth goes too deep, these days, news travels too fast and wide for myths to hold their substance long.

So you are taking your destiny into your own hands.

The realization that we are just one dot in the universe, that we are not its hub—or (probably) the most intelligent creatures in it—should *not* make you want to cry despondently, 'Ah, then we don't matter?'

We should welcome the discovery of truth. This is our age—and that means it is the age of truth. And the clear knowledge of what we are—our identity in relation to the universe of which we are so small a part—should fill us with delight. The very nature of our being, as we know it now, shows us that we are not some bauble in the hands of fate or of a mystic purpose over which we have no control. We, collectively, are like a party of mountaineers or explorers coping with the terrain and conditions in which we find ourselves. *Our future is in our hands alone. It is up to us: we are the masters of our fate!*

To recognize this is not to feel 'lost'. Far from it!

On the other hand, it does provide an enormously strengthened argument that we should know ourselves, our potentials and our motivations: that we should thereby be in a position to measure ourselves against the universe in which our lives and futures are bound, and into which, like surgeons discovering new life-saving techniques, we probe more deeply all the time.

With technological advance comes heightened responsibility. As I just said—we have to take our destinies into our own hands. We have to assume the responsibilities for our own actions. We know, now, that there are no hands other than ours to carry it. The more power we have, the more self-control and self-direction we will need to use that power constructively.

So naturally the old standards are questioned. *Of course* the 'commandments' and moralities of bygone ages must be inspected, overhauled and in some cases thrown out. It isn't enough to be told what's right and what's wrong: you must see the reasons. And as soon as you start looking, you stumble up against ancient pillars of morality which often are no more than hindrances, in mid-thoroughfare, to the fast-moving streams of modern thought. Sometimes there are even rules which, in practical terms and in relation to a standard which insists on *honesty in personal relationships* as a basis for the moral viewpoint, make for *immorality*.

You should not, in an age of self-awareness, accept rules or principles which cause suffering, indignity or despair. You should not accept any standard which obscures the truth.

Now in order to establish *new* standards, you must experiment, explore, discuss and discover. This is the stage through which we are passing now. And if you are one of those who view our present social tendencies —or, admittedly, confusions—with alarm or despair, who wail that there are now no standards of behaviour (political, sexual, etc.) and that only degradation and ruin face the human race, consider this:

(*a*) We are not losing standards—but replacing outworn standards with others which relate more closely to human needs.

(b) They will be based on our needs, capacity and potential—and honesty in our relationships with others.

(c) Relaxing the influence of religion does *not* mean there will be no more moral standards left! Moral order and ethical precepts provided the basic structure of primitive societies long before the arrival of any 'formal' religion. In fact anthropologists have learned that religion was often superimposed on the natural social orders, being brought in to reinforce with mystical authority the practical rules first made for social or even hygienic purposes. An obvious example is to be found in some of the *Kosher* laws of the Jewish faith.

(d) 'Morals' often possess no deeper meaning than 'customs'. One thinks, for instance, of marriage customs in certain African and Polynesian tribes: customs very different from ours, but possibly productive of a higher standard of morality. It is the behaviour of one human being towards another that counts more than any rule of procedure.

By morality I'm not talking specifically about sex any more than I'm thinking particularly of business, space exploration or the arts. But as an example of morals/customs gone mad, consider the Victorian households in which piano legs had to be hidden, for the sake of decency, in little 'trousers'!

Passing from the silly to the horrible, consider the eighteen-year-old girl who, in something like three average life-times ago, was publicly burned to death in the Strand, London, for refusing to believe that the bread of Holy Communion changed to the flesh of Christ in the moment of its being consumed.

Of course we have to turn our backs on the past, re-think our human role and standards. But change, the need to revalue, doesn't leave you in a vacuum, any more than it leaves you without morals. On the contrary—it presents you with vast new opportunities for your own self-fulfilment.

It presents you with real freedom—the right to accept responsibility for your own actions. *If you are to measure up to that responsibility, self-knowledge is a pre-requisite.*

And in the context of this freedom, we must for our own protection establish a new and realistic moral order. The basis of any such code in the climate of today is consideration by each individual of the feelings, needs and emotions of every other individual with whom he or she is in relationship. And how can you effectively show an unselfish consideration of other people's feelings unless you are able to understand them? Unless you know what they want as well as you know what you want for yourself?

How original is sin?

The Church tells you, you were born in sin. That man is inherently sinful. 'Original' sin, they call it.

To shift the emphasis slightly, have you noticed the wistful adoration in people's faces (women especially) when they look at a small, new baby? Have you ever wondered *why* they think it's 'sweet'?

Well, I'll tell you. It's because they're looking at *innocence*. At a pure heart and fresh eyes and a clean slate—none of which will ever be quite so pure, fresh on clean again. This is what wrings your heart, even makes you want to cry.

'Original sin', my foot!

But with this background of drip-feed guilt, indoctrination, it's not surprising that you have a sense of 'sin' or inferiority bred into you, so that at the slightest stirring of conscience—or unfounded accusation!—you hear a trembling voice deep inside you whisper, 'Yes, I'm guilty!'

It's a load of rubbish. A ploy to keep the congregation with their knees on the cold stone floor and their eyes down in humility and contrition. But it's more than a load of rubbish—it's a load of *dangerous* rubbish!

Remember how Omar Khayyám expressed the doubt? The way he put it, according to Edward Fitzgerald, was

> Oh Thou who didst with Pitfall and with Gin
> Beset the road I was to wander in,
> Thou wilt not with Predestination round
> Enmesh me, and impute my Fall to Sin?

An understandable doubt, and a reasonable hope. If you dig a bear-trap in the garden path where your wife takes her evening stroll, and she falls into it, are you going to accuse her of being clumsy?

The deliberate implantation of a sense of guilt in the human mind is, in my opinion, a crime against humanity. It may date from the story of Adam and Eve; but however great your personal faith you won't surely accept *everything* you read in the Scriptures. Even a bishop, I imagine, would find it difficult to applaud the order to Saul to 'go and smite Amalek, and utterly destroy all that they have, and spare them not; but slay both man and woman, infant and suckling . . .'

The bishop couldn't applaud that any more than he could support the edicts of Adolf Hitler. The Pope *did* have a medal struck to celebrate the cold-blooded massacre of 20,000 Protestants, of course—but that was back in 1572. Our bishop, if he had to comment on what the Lord spelled out to Amalek, would probably say that the story should be seen in the context of the savage times from which it originated. Well, all right—you can forget it, and forget about Adam and Eve too, and use the saved time to concentrate on the needs of *today*.

And the fact is this: you have enough problems and frailties of your own without having artificial ones injected into your psychological veins. Developing personalities need encouragement, injections of hope and purpose: not disparagement and counsels of despair!

Banish—reject absolutely—those feelings of guilt. You were born with clean hands and a clean record. If you've 'sinned' since, the odds are that you've made up for it. The certainty is that mental sackcloth and ashes won't even help to keep your hair tidy.

Tell yourself this:

I was born innocent. I'm no angel now—I'm a human being. I'm bound to 'go wrong' sometimes; that's part of living, and living is what I'm here for!

Don't test the water with your toe and then draw back

Don't be scared of getting hurt. Don't be frightened of shocks to your emotional system. They are as much a part of you as your arms and legs. Like arms and legs, they need using, exercising.

If you don't use *all* your muscles, some will fall into disuse, and your body will no longer be the balanced, healthy machine it could have been.

The muscles of your emotional self need flexing too. If you guard them in a kind of mental refrigerator to protect them (protect yourself) from hurt, you'll be only half-living, half-aware. You may be avoiding the possibility of pain, but in fact you're avoiding life itself. How can you care for *any* machinery by letting it grind to a halt and rust?

You can't make an omelette without breaking eggs. You have to fire a shot before you can correct your aim. *To live, you must experience life.* Don't be afraid to *feel*—to *react*—to suffer, if necessary.

Love—fear—feeling—anger—pleasure—pain—they're all part of living.

You're going to die, one day. When the time comes, which do you want to be most aware of—

how much you've missed?

or

*how much you've **lived**?*